A GUIDE TO GETTING ALONG IN THE CORPORATE AGE

THE NEW OFFICE ETIQUETTE

George Mazzei

POSEIDON PRESS

NEW YORK

A Poseidon Press Book
Published by Pocket Books,
A Simon & Schuster Division of Gulf & Western Corporation
Simon & Schuster Building
Rockefeller Center
1230 Avenue of the Americas
New York, New York 10020

POSEIDON PRESS is a trademark of Simon & Schuster
Designed by Irving Perkins Associates
Manufactured in the United States of America
10 9 8 7 6 5 4 3 2 1

Library of Congress Cataloging in Publication Data

Mazzei, George.
    The new office etiquette.

    Includes index.
    1. Business etiquette.   I. Title.
HF5387.M39   1983   395'.52   82-18951
ISBN 0-671-45407-2

ACKNOWLEDGMENTS

THE AUTHOR WISHES to thank the following people for their help, opinions and advice in preparing this book: Jacqueline Booker, fashion consultant; Brian Burdine, creative director; Edward Lee Cave, corporate executive; Thomas M Conway, financial administrator; Robert Dahlin, managing editor and writer; Joelle Delbourgo, book editor and executive; Humphrey Evans, literary agent; Charles Hix, writer and journalist; Rick Horton, lawyer; Constance Kelly, development consultant; Eleanor Kozlofsky, secretary; Arlene Lefkowitz, secretary; Al Madocs, executive assistant; Bob Patino, interior designer; Kenn G. Pointer, account controller; Hugh Stanford Porter, bank vice-president; Roger Sharpe, corporate vice-president; Alice Smith, editor; Aileen Stein, free-lance writer and editor; Mary Ann Stuart, corporate vice-president; John R. Sullivan, publicity director; Holmes Tuttle, executive and businessman; Sondra Vedock, educational director; John Weitz, designer.

We wish to thank, too, the people who gave their time to helping prepare this book but who preferred to be anonymous. The kindness and cordiality of all of you is greatly appreciated.

THIS BOOK IS FOR JOHN R. SULLIVAN, IN GRATITUDE FOR HIS generosity in sharing his knowledge, his contacts, and his many experiences where etiquette saved the day

CONTENTS

INTRODUCTION 11

1 COMING, GOING, AND SETTLING IN 15

2 AT HOME IN THE OFFICE 33

3 STYLES AND SENSIBILITIES 65

4 WOMEN AT WORK 100

5 WHEN CUPID GETS STUPID 116

6 A GOOD "GIRL" IS HARD TO FIND 144

7 THE BOSS MYSTIQUE 167

8 A CALL IS WAITING 188

9 WINING, DINING, AND DECLINING 208

10 NEW WAVES AND FREE AGENTS 233

11 THE TRAVELING BUSINESS 238

FINALE 249

INDEX 251

INTRODUCTION

THERE WAS A time not so long ago when etiquette was an essential part of one's equipment for getting ahead in the business world. Everyone was expected to behave politely toward one another, whether it was the president of the company talking to the mail-boy, a factory worker talking to her co-worker at the brewery, or the milkman delivering the butter and eggs. Everyone felt the need to follow certain patterns of considerate interaction when doing business of any kind.

Lately there is a feeling that this system of etiquette has broken down. People seem to be more rude with one another in every sector of society; as a result, many people feel a need for clear guidelines on how to act in the office or in any situation having to do with their jobs.

The business situation is more or less a stepchild of "real" life. You spend the best hours of the best days of your life in intimate nonrelationships with people who have little in common with you beyond working for the same company. If you get another job tomorrow, you will walk out of their lives without a backward glance at these people you've lived with for quite a long time.

Almost all corporate situations involve a social interaction of some sort, whether it's a business lunch with a client, a good-bye party for the silver-haired receptionist, a discreet blindness to the boss's mistress, or just getting along with an office smoker, a grouch, or an obnoxiously vivacious creative director. Since there is very

11

little left of what used to be called basic good manners and so much has changed in the structure of the typical business situation, there is a clear-cut need for new guidelines and ground rules for getting along.

The best way to conduct your business life is to keep a clear dividing line between personal and professional affairs, but apart from word processors and computers no thinking entity can really do that. Even Ebenezer Scrooge had to let up on the pressure eventually and go buy Tiny Tim a goose. We are humans all the time; only workaholics turn off the emotions and work like automatons. We must apply the same rules of getting along with people to office life that we apply to "real" life.

When you must contact people outside the company, you are expected to court them, almost as if you were cultivating a new friend or even a lover. Since such courting in business is done for mercenary reasons, you can't rely on playing these artificial situations by ear. Your career may depend on how well you can run a smooth course through waters that are often frequented by schools of corporate barracuda.

In the past ten years women have taken an equal position in the business world with men, and there have been many changes in the prevailing business atmosphere. During the sixties, if a twenty-seven-year-old woman was making a hundred thousand dollars a year her name was probably Sandra Dee. Today women are no longer merely adjuncts to men's careers; women are bosses, competitors, colleagues—and, to many men who don't know how to relate to them in these new roles, they are also puzzlements. The old system of courtly deference to women no longer applies when you're both rushing for the same taxicab. New definitions are needed in the interrelations between men and women in business.

The telephone has become as much a part of business in our multinational commercial world as the typewriter. Most executives conduct at least 50 percent of their business on the phone. Some executives receive as many as two hundred phone calls a day. Since so much depends on the way we use this instrument, we must be careful not to ruin things through unconscious gaffes on the phone.

Young people are coming into business today without much

background in good manners. It is useless to deny the fact that a whole generation has grown up without being given much training in the use of the words "Please," "Thank you," and "Excuse me." Even people in their mid-thirties complain about this abrupt gap in American manners. Because things have changed so radically from a male-dominated to a shared corporate structure, because there is so much money to be made by very young talented people, because there is so much job switching that goes on, and because things have changed so tremendously so quickly, there is a real need for guidelines for business behavior.

We need to deal with the ambiguities in business today without taking up a lot of time learning through guesswork. Business etiquette is the key. We need clear directions to take us through a situation where men can be receptionists and secretaries; where a twenty-seven-year-old woman may hire a thirty-five-year-old man to work for her; where a corporation vice-president can show up at work in Levi's in one town, while a twenty-two-year-old junior exec in another place has to cut off his beard to keep his job.

In the main, we can no longer apply the same standards and requirements for behavior in business that were common twenty years ago. Rigid codes no longer work because no one wants to live that way anymore. Employee rights now have at least the same importance in business as corporate requirements. Arbitrary demands for employees to adhere to a certain company image don't make sense anymore. People work for themselves in their own minds, and guidelines for dress and behavior must have a basis in logic or they won't be followed.

You can, for example, require an employee in a legal firm to wear a suit and tie at work, because a certain image is necessary for the company's survival. But to ask a woman secretary in an automobile sales garage not to wear a pantsuit would be a futile exercise in tyranny.

The etiquette decisions presented in this book are based on interviews with a variety of working people at all levels, and on commonsense decent treatment and consideration of one person for another. Some things have not changed at all since the Eisenhower years; other things that are now commonplace would make a Wall Streeter from the fifties cringe further into his button-down collar.

Today's business etiquette arises from the situation as it is and must provide space for individual creativity, idiosyncrasy, and preference. The guidelines in this book reflect the general current trend in thinking and are based on the idea that individual behavior should come out of mutual respect, self-control, and a sublimation of egotism. Etiquette exists primarily to make things easier in business, to improve everyone's enjoyment of the time spent at work, and to help people perform the function of business more efficiently.

Etiquette rules are not laws handed down from on high. When the time arises, etiquette must be set aside for business survival. The idea of dying for honor doesn't hold here. Etiquette is a tool that is good only as long as it helps to achieve a goal. This does not mean that rudeness would at times be preferable; nasty behavior never serves any function in business. It does mean that when you are used to living by a code of interpersonal respect and consideration you will know automatically how to react without having to look it up in the rulebook.

Good manners, my first boss told me, are a natural outgrowth of self-respect. They don't have to be taught if you remember to treat others with the same consideration you would expect from them. I hope that this set of guidelines will provide a groundwork for that attitude to become part of your career.

1

COMING, GOING, AND SETTLING IN

BY TAKING the right approach from the start, when you're just looking for a job, you can guarantee that things will go smoothly when you're actually working. So many people approach the task of job hunting with such feelings of insecurity, inadequacy, and confusion that it's a wonder they get hired at all. The situation is further complicated because many people don't know how to handle job applicants. Getting jobs, settling into them, and eventually leaving them all call for delicacy and discretion in behavior. If you start off on the right foot, you will have better working relationships. If you leave a job with positive feelings, it can only enhance your reputation and increase your career opportunities.

THE RÉSUMÉ

Some cynics have said that a good résumé isn't worth the paper it's printed on. All it does, they say, is give an employer something

15

to do with his hands while the applicant fumbles for words. This is not a fair estimation. A good résumé gets you the interview, so you can get the job. It should provide a clear picture of your experience so the employer can decide if it's worth getting to know more about you.

When seeking a job interview, send your résumé with a covering letter to make things more personal. The letter should reflect something of your personality while being brief and to the point. In it you say you are enclosing the résumé and ask for an interview. You may also suggest that you will call within a week and see if a time can be arranged for the requested interview.

When you send a résumé in response to a classified ad, the cover letter should specify which job you are applying for. If the ad says "Résumés Only," a letter is not needed. It is a sign of anxiety to try to "overkill" by sending more than the ad asks for, and also bad manners since the employer will be inundated with résumés and any extra reading matter may not be welcome. If your résumé is good enough, it can stand alone before a discerning employer.

It is bad manners for the recipient of an unsolicited résumé to ignore it. Some response, even a refusal of an interview, is required. If the applicant is contacting the employer under a referral, it is even more imperative to acknowledge it, and an interview is mandatory. It is bad manners to undercut a colleague who is referring someone to you for an interview. If the interview is impossible, a kind, personal letter should be sent to the applicant, and the referring party must also be given an explanation.

If the résumés come in response to an ad, it is not necessary to contact any except those you wish to interview. Applicants who answer "blind" ads do so with the understanding that they may not be right for the job and may never be contacted.

Any applicant who has been interviewed must be notified within a short time about his status. If he is no longer being considered, a polite letter expressing thanks for his time and regrets that he cannot be taken on should be sent.

The time limit for responding to any applicant who answers an ad or who has been interviewed should be no longer than two weeks. No applicant should be left hanging if there is a possibility that he may be seriously considered for a job. It marks a lack of professionalism to take a leisurely amount of time before contacting an applicant.

If you know on the spot that an applicant is wrong for the job, it is best to inform the person at that time rather than waiting. This information will free him to consider other possibilities.

It is a duty of the employer to return any materials to applicants that are needed for further job hunting. You keep the résumé, but documents, clippings, and references must be returned to the applicant. You can cause much damage and expense by not doing this. Early in my career, I applied for a writing job with the United Fund and naively submitted my entire portfolio. The interviewer threw it away and never bothered to inform me of my chances for the job. The damage was compounded by the usual lie—"We sent the material back to you." I never got it and was unable to replace most of it, since I had moved to another town. You should never tie up anyone's portfolio for longer than three days, unless the applicant assures you that it makes no difference how long you keep it.

THE INTERVIEW

It is a toss-up about which is the least fun: being interviewed for a job or having to interview applicants who want a job. Rarely is there that fabled successful interview where the talk comes easily, immediate rapport is established, and the person turns out to be perfect for the job.

Today there are plenty of people interviewing job applicants who are not really capable of evaluating their skills. There are also people who do not know the proper things to do and say at a job interview that will convey to the interviewer what he really wants to know. What people really want to know in the short time you have together is simply, Who is the real you and what are you like to work with? All the professional information on your résumé will tell what you have done and what you can reasonably be expected to do.

The employer should try to make some set of guidelines for himself or herself about what is desired in a person for a certain job. It is very difficult to gauge a person in an interview, but I have always found that you will have an undeniable spark of liking for the person if he or she is right—independent of experience or résumé.

The two best people I ever hired had no résumés at all. I interviewed them with my boss. The first one we hired was a twenty-two-year-old graduate who was so shy she couldn't say much and had absolutely no experience except in the accounting department. We merely fell in love with her and knew that she couldn't fail. She turned out to be better than any other associate editor we ever had—including me.

The second one came into the office and never said anything except, "I need a job, and you're going to hire me because I'm the best person you can possibly get. So quit wasting your time and hire me." We were so dazzled we never said a word except, "We have to discuss it and let you know."

She never stopped dazzling or talking. On her way out she said in ringing tones, "Now, call me tomorrow . . . and hire me! I'll be waiting." I escorted her to the elevators, more because I wanted to than from any point of etiquette. When I came back in, everyone was looking at me with bemused, "Who was that?" looks on their faces. My boss was standing, gloriously happy, smiling out the window. I looked at him.

He said, "Tell me why we *shouldn't* hire her. Just tell me why we shouldn't hire her!"

What could I say? I called her that day and told her to get herself into the office tomorrow.

That's how we always decided—on cold, hard, businesslike . . . emotional response.

When interviewing an applicant, an employer should extend full business and professional courtesy. This is especially important because the person being interviewed is likely to be extremely tense. Whatever you can do to make an applicant feel more relaxed should be done. An offer of coffee or tea is always welcome and makes the person feel he or she is dealing with a human being.

The interviewer should try to set the same tone that the person will find in the office when and if he or she starts to work there. If the atmosphere is formal and muted, act that way. If it is loose and casual, then make it known. Do not be so loose and casual that the person is incited to act foolish, however. You are still conducting an interview and need information about the applicant.

Present an accurate picture of the job and its good and bad points. Do not tell an applicant that a job will lead to the "possibility" of doing other things "if it works out." If it does work out and the person can be given greater creative opportunities, then give them. But don't make vague promises at an interview. For some reason the applicant is most likely to hook on to those statements as promises, and they will come back to haunt you.

If it is bad practice for an employer to hold a carrot on a stick before applicants, it is bad policy to take a job based on a promise of what it could lead to or the promise of getting a raise in six months if things work out. You must consider the job at hand and decide if you want to do it as part of your career. It is true that some jobs are stepping-stones to higher things, but you still have to deal with the position you are applying for. In business, promises have a way of evaporating as the economy fluctuates.

On the other hand, if the job is designed to be held by someone who is not looking for a brilliant career, it is best to say that the position is for someone who wants to do it, and only it, for as long as possible.

HOW TO DRESS

The employer should wear the same clothes that are acceptable any other time in the office. Applicants must wing it, unless the interviewer has specifically said that dressing up is not necessary for the interview. It may be somewhat of a jolt to an anxious applicant dressed up in a suit and tie and pocket handkerchief to enter an office and find everyone else slumming it in jeans and T-shirts. If that is the policy, the applicant should be informed ahead of time.

If unsure of what to wear, remember that a suit and tie for men, and businesslike dresses or suits for women, are never objection-able. Normal conservative attire always works for first-time meetings of any kind.

THE DRIPS

It is difficult to be polite to applicants who drag themselves in, disgusted at the prospect of yet another job interview, but it can be done. You listen to them, ask them some questions, wait for some sign of life, and if there is none, slap them awake, thank them, and send them away. I always tell these people that I don't think they are right for the job and let it go at that. And wish them luck—they'll need it.

THE PESTS

More difficult are the ones who are not right for the job but want it anyway. I had one man call and beg me for an interview because he wanted to get into fashion writing. He was, at the time, making more money than I was, but he wanted to back up and take a job as a beginning proofreader. I explained that the job wouldn't take him where he wanted to go and certainly wouldn't give me the future editor I was looking for. He was persistent and kept calling to see if I'd changed my mind. I tried to refer him to places where he might conceivably get a foothold in the fashion business; I even asked our own fashion director to see him. But he didn't want to work in the fashion department, so I stopped helping.

Persistent applicants who already know they have no chance at a job remove themselves from the etiquette lineup. It is rude in the extreme to be a pest in a business situation. It is not necessary to accept or return calls from such an applicant. If you wish to save yourself or your secretary the hassle of dealing with him, you might refer him to a job that he might fill. Once you have done this favor, it is likely that the pest will quit bothering you. If you are referring him to someone you know well, however, forewarn that person of your experience. If the job actually works out well, you will have gained a friend who owes you a business favor.

AFTER THE INTERVIEW

Do not pester an employer for a job. No one can manufacture a job just because you want one. It is all right to check back several months after an interview to see if there are any openings, but after six months of no response it makes you look like a loser to be calling about the same job. The employer will wonder what is wrong with you if you are still hanging on his goodwill; or, worse, he may feel sorry for you. It is important to present an image of self-sufficiency when job hunting. People are attracted to success and can read it on you. It is bad manners to cry the blues to an employer. Do not tell him how difficult it is to find a job. Everyone knows that. Stick to the facts of what you can offer him and what he can offer you.

Some employers see it as an annoyance to receive follow-up letters from people they have interviewed for jobs. Others see it as a special touch, an indication that you really want to work for that company and are not just looking for any job. The applicant must decide whether or not to do this. It is never rude to do so, and if you are really right for the job, and the interviewer liked you already, it will most likely be a point in your favor.

If you do not feel the interview went well, it is not good to ask for another interview. Remember that first impressions are important. If you do not come off well the first time, it is not likely that you will be able to overcome the negative impression by asking for a second try.

It is up to the employer to determine if the applicant has been interviewed at a disadvantage. If the employer feels a second interview might provide a better picture by which to evaluate the applicant, it is his prerogative to invite the applicant back. No matter what the circumstances, the applicant cannot take the initiative here. Comfort lies in the fact that if an interviewer is not discerning enough to determine how fair the interview was, the company probably is a bad one to work for anyway.

If ten days pass and you have not heard from an interviewer, it is acceptable to call and ask whether or not the job is still open. In my own experience, if I had not done this I would not have known I had a job. My phone was out of order and I didn't know it, being new to town and having few friends. When I called my prospective employers back to check out my status, I was informed that they were just about to give up on me because they couldn't reach me. From a practical point of view, there is no reason to avoid double-checking after an interview.

BLIND HUNT

It is correct for a person interested in working for a particular company to make an inquiry by letter (not by telephone) to an appropriate person. Many employers like to meet new talent for future reference, even if nothing is available at the moment. Many times these meetings can be very fruitful. I know several people who were hired through these "over the transom" requests. It is common sense and courtesy for anyone who can spare the time to meet new people this way—especially in the creative fields. It prevents tunnel vision.

ARRIVING

When starting at a new job, it is best to be somewhat reserved in order to get a feel of the place and a sense of the kind of people who work there, and, to state it baldly, to learn how far to trust them. Too many people are too exuberant at first in an attempt to be liked. It is best to listen as much as possible, get a hook on office procedure, and learn who not to make friends with. If you are coming in at a beginning position, this will be the best way to gain the goodwill of established co-workers; if you are coming into a position of authority, it allows you to objectively gauge the people who will report to you. It is not fair to the people already there to rush them into a judgment on you. Both sides need time to get acquainted.

LEGACIES

The inherited secretary, associate executive, staff, or assistant is a common problem among executives. Even if the people are talented, they may not be compatible with the new order, or they may not fit into a new boss's new vision. It is always pleasant when an executive finds he or she can keep on an inherited secretary; it certainly can expedite putting one's ideas into practice to have an experienced assistant ready to go; but such luck is not common.

Any person coming on in a new position of authority does best to maintain a polite but discreet distance and make no promises at the start. If you want someone of your own choice in the job of assistant or close associate, you should make that clear; but if you are not decided on what your action will be, then you must say nothing one way or the other.

If you feel a person will not work out with you, it is best to say so early, to enable the person to relocate without a break in employment. If there is a possibility of transferring the person to another spot in the company, it should be explored. Any person who is going to be let go because of a change and not because of incompetence must be given an especially long period to find another position. He or she must also be allowed a reasonable amount of office time to go on interviews. If this is not possible, then the person let go should be given extra severance pay.

MONEY SPEAKS

The first rule of etiquette concerning your income is never tell anyone except your mate and the IRS. Some people don't even tell them. You are paid based on various factors: when you started with the company, how much it could get away with paying you and keeping you, how much your job is getting on the overall market, how valuable you are to the company.

It should make no difference to you what another person in your position is receiving. It has nothing to do with you. The old cry about equal pay for equal work is debilitating in the corporate structure. It squelches the intramural competition that keeps individual talent alive. If you want more money, fight for it on your own merits; don't go whining like a kid to his mother that someone else is getting a bigger piece of cake. Fairness has little to do with salaries at the executive level. Creativity and the ability to convince your company that you are worth any amount are the only factors that should be considered.

WHAT ARE YOU WORTH?

Everyone has a sense that he or she is worth more than the after-tax amount on each paycheck. When asking for a raise, it is important to know how much to go for and when to hold off. There used to be a scale for executives to go by which said you should be making $10,000 for each decade of your life. That meant that someone in his twenties should be making $20,000; a thirty-year-old should be getting $30,000; and so on till retirement. Pure fiction, of course, since many executives were retiring at $30,000 or $40,000, and few young people could command more than $15,000 or $18,000 at the most.

The best way to find out if your own salary is commensurate with the going rate in your professional and age group is to ask around. You cannot, of course, get together with a colleague for lunch and ask point-blank, "How much do you make?" You can, however, ask, "What is the going salary for someone in my position?" You can also call around and ask for salary levels at specific corporations. You can always say that you're interested in getting into that company but aren't sure it would be worthwhile financially to leave your current job.

Salary levels are often common knowledge. If you ask five people, you can be pretty sure of obtaining a correct picture of your own comparative income expectations. One of the best and most accurate ways to learn is to register with employment agencies and find out from them what you are worth, based on your experience, the reputation of your company, and what they think they can get for you based on current demand for people in your field. The best way to get an *in*accurate picture is to read the classified ads. The salaries in them are usually either overinflated or depressingly understated, depending on the impression the advertiser wants to convey.

PROMISES, PROMISES

When you are promised a raise and it never materializes, it is necessary to be firm and demanding. Many companies consider raises after six months for new employees. Often when the six months are up the company balks at coming through. It is best to have a firm promise on paper at the start, or to get the money up front, before accepting the job. Do not ever take less money on the promise of more to come when you prove yourself. If a company cannot evaluate your merits on your experience and take the risk, you will find much to be unhappy about.

No company should promise a raise in a certain time period, but companies should review employees' salaries regularly. Too many people go to work angry and frustrated over false promises of money, especially after they've left another job on the basis of that promise. It is better to bull it through at your present job than to take another one for promised future money. Usually it will not materialize. You are only a star once, and you will never have the clout of newness again.

STAYING ALIVE

If you stay with one company for a long period of time, you are likely to fall behind in salary advancement. Companies must pay more to get new talent each year as the market changes; but they often maintain scaled incremental advancement for established employees. If you want more money, it is best to move around. One economist told me that you should never let your love of a job keep you back. It is a fact of corporate life that the longer you stay put, the more your salary stays put with you.

If you want to get more money and are falling below what you feel you should earn based on your age and the job market, then you must take some action and ask for a raise. It is always best to have reliable information on hand before asking for more money from your company. If you find you are underpaid, you should discuss the matter with your immediate boss. There may be a reason. If you feel the reason is not valid, then perhaps you'd better take steps to reevaluate your whole approach to your career. Many of us get into ruts and don't know it. Many of us have personality problems that hinder our advancement and we are not made aware of them. There are many self-improvement groups geared to executives, and there is a very good reason for them. Too many people advance on guesswork, and if you aren't a good guesser, you may not get ahead.

The best approach to a boss who gives you a mediocre report on your abilities is first to consider his remarks objectively and decide if they have validity. Secondly, you must evaluate your boss's motives. Many people maintain their own positions by keeping other people insecure while utilizing their abilities to bolster their own careers. It is a common practice to make people think they aren't worth much, refuse them raises, and give them the impression that their work is somehow below par—all for the purpose of keeping talented but naive people from getting ahead. It is a survival trick. Always make sure your boss is not this kind of person before taking all of his or her comments as gospel truth.

Never give your employer an ultimatum; it alienates his goodwill and causes resentment. Some, given an ultimatum about money or leaving, will tell you they're sorry to see you go. An ultimatum from a longtime employee tends to be taken as an affront, even when the person has a valid point to make about his income. If you make an ultimatum, then back down when it doesn't work, you will never have any clout again, and you will have a black mark against you in your employer's mind. It is fair to persist in requests for raises, but don't make threats. Provide reasons and present evidence of need if necessary, but an ultimatum is strictly out of line.

The best approach is to look for another job quietly, and when an offer is made, either take it or use it as a lever to obtain a substantial raise. Oddly, many companies will let you go and pay a new person even more than you requested rather than give in to pressure. It sets a precedent for other employees and can become expensive. Never become resentful, because this seeming unfairness is a necessary part of keeping the company solvent. Utilize only legitimate business tactics to gain your money.

Don't suggest that you are receiving nibbles from other companies unless you have an actual offer *that you would like to accept.* If you are important enough, it will become known through rumor and scare your own company into wooing you before you consider moving. If your company is willing to let you go, then you should go—even if you prefer to stay. The company does not think of you as important and you will not get the advancement you will want.

BEING JEALOUS

It happens that you think you deserve a raise and/or a promotion but the company hires someone from outside. This type of occurence must be swallowed gracefully. If you feel you should have been considered and weren't, you can make inquiries to see if perhaps you are failing and don't know it. It may be simply that someone high up in the company has some plan in mind and the new person can best facilitate it.

No one has a right to grouse and complain around the office if he or she has been passed over. The only acceptable course of action is to ask for a meeting with the appropriate superior and take his comments for what they are. Perhaps you have a valid complaint and it will be recognized and the situation amended in some way. If not, the previously suggested course of action—either looking elsewhere for work or taking some business improvement courses—is advisable.

Business is not always fair. It does what is most expedient at times and often appears brutal or unfair in the process. It is also possible that someone will benefit from a seeming pass-over because it will spark him to improve, or to get a job in a company where his talents will be appreciated more. Always consider that you may not be in the right place at the right time in cases like this. No one has the right to expect a raise or job based on etiquette; always keep evaluating your talents, your position, and whether or not you are getting in a rut. What was the right company for you in your third career year may be the wrong one two years later. Weigh all considerations before getting depressed or feeling wronged.

INNER TRANSFER

Often, employees wish to improve their job position by moving within the company. It makes sense because they are already established and known and have proved themselves. They are familiar with the company policies and have an advantage over any new person who may come from outside. They are, in short, already broken in.

If you want to make such a move, there is an etiquette involved, based on your responsibility to your present boss. You can feel out the possibility of your qualifying for the other job through your personnel department or through the person who would be your new boss. If you find the move a likely prospect, you must discuss your desire to transfer with your present boss. You have an obligation to try to get his or her blessing, whether or not you do transfer. Present your ambitions clearly and professionally; keep the reasons strictly impersonal. It is then up to the boss to extend you the courtesy of wishing you good luck. It is extremely bad manners to make it difficult for an employee to move on to another position he or she may be happier in.

If one has a good, open relationship with the boss, it is possible to discuss the desire for a job in another department and ask for his or her help in making the transfer. It is usually the better policy, however, to make sure your application would be considered before telling your own boss. In this case, the nature of a person's relationship with his or her boss is the deciding factor.

LETTING GO

The time comes for every star to burn out, and in business we find that stars "go nova" when asked to follow this natural rule. Talented people often are asked to move on to better positions and leave their star-status position behind for someone else to fill. It has always seemed odd to me that these supertalents don't realize that they made the job such a plum, rather than being a star because of the job. In any event, it's extremely difficult even in nonfamous cases to get a valuable employee to move on to some job where he or she is needed and give up the star job. He or she usually wants to take the new job as well as to control the person doing the old one.

It is never good manners to want to control your old job. In business you cannot have the idea that any job or company is "yours"; when the last line is drawn it is just a business after all, and a tool by which whoever needs an income can make one. People must accept the passage of time and make room for new people.

It is also not good manners to go back to a place where one worked brilliantly and make comparisons. People have their own jobs to do, and they like to think they are doing things well their way. Always remember that a job exists only in the present, and it "belongs" to whoever is getting paid to do it.

GOING

The time always comes to say good-bye to a company and to the people you worked with there. The reasons for your leaving should be kept private, for the most part. It is perfectly all right to say you are leaving for a better position, or because you need a sabbatical, or for reasons of health. If these are not the reasons, it is best to pick one of them anyway.

Our favorite secretary decided to leave because she wanted to live in Hawaii. We offered to let her take six months to change her mind and come back to us, but she said no to that, and we decided not to press. Unfortunately, when she came back anyway we had a secretary we couldn't let go because she was as good. But Marion really did want a change. Hawaii was only an indication of a changing attitude.

It is always polite to leave the door open to people who might seem to want to return if it is possible and desirable to do so. It is not polite to badger them about the possibility. Even the best of friends have to part, and a person who has no point of dissatisfaction with a job may have very private reasons for leaving. It could be something as simple as not being able to meet marriageable people. Do not go around threatening to quit your job behind your boss's back. If you seriously want to leave, look for a new job and do it. It is counterproductive and demoralizing to have a staff person making such statements. Since office morale is extremely important to a company, such action is proper grounds for dismissal.

It is also extremely wrong to make an office a battleground during an interoffice power struggle. It places other people in a bad position and frightens them, since one person's demise may take a whole department as well. Political games, dissatisfaction with employees, disenchantment with the job—all are things to be discussed with the proper person and are not matters for grousing, coffee-break bitching, or publicly discrediting another person in the company.

If you have been fired, or plan to fire someone, this should be kept as private a matter as possible. If you are doing the firing, do not let it be known to other staff people that the person is on the way out, unless you want to feel someone out as a replacement.

MOVING ON

It happens often that someone who has a job wants to move on. This should be done quietly, since many companies will fire employees who are job hunting. The best way to arrange such matters is through discreet phone calls, lunch dates, and inquiries among business friends. The reason for discretion is more political than mannerly: you will not want to reveal your hand before you play it.

QUITTING

It is common courtesy when you leave a job to let the company know in advance. But you should always discuss it privately with your immediate boss first. It is also common courtesy to offer several weeks' notice so the company won't be left in a bind. Some people leave after being refused a raise, feeling that they should not have to give up the extra money for two weeks. This is rude behavior, but it may be acceptable to the employer who doesn't want a disgruntled employee hanging around spreading gloom.

One of the crudest things I ever witnessed occurred when a friend quit his job as a publicity director to take a better offer. The new job dissolved, but his company would not let him stay on in his position. The reasoning was that he was looking for a new job. Sorry reasoning: everyone is always looking for a better job in theory—that's just good business. The company had to run crippled until a new person could establish himself in the job and to bear the expense of closing the former employee out.

HOUSECLEANING

It is fair to reevaluate your staff periodically with an eye to replacing people who should move on. In some businesses which need to change with the times or the economy—especially creative fields—these decisions are commonplace. Some people use this as an excuse to wield an ax, but it is undeniable that some companies require the influx of new creative talent to survive.

In these cases the people earmarked for dismissal should be forewarned to give them a running chance to find new positions, in or out of the company.

TWO WEEKS' NOTICE

People who have been dismissed should be permitted to continue at work for two weeks only if they do not lay a cloud of complaints and bitterness over the office. The usual thing is to give two weeks' notice in the form of severance pay, and let them tie up details. This is the best policy and saves the most embarrassment for all. It seems odd that a highly paid exec should be able to leave his job at a moment's notice, but the reality remains—he can. He doesn't take the company down with him.

THE JOB SUIT

If an employee brings a lawsuit against the company or against a person in the company, it should be determined by the plaintiff's lawyer and the company's lawyers whether or not the plaintiff should remain on the job until the case is settled. If a secretary is suing her boss for sexual harassment, for example, it may be impossible for them to maintain the kind of relationship necessary for expediting the work. If she can be transferred to another department or to another executive's office, it should be arranged. There may not be any reason why a person suing the company cannot continue to perform, since there may not be any actual personality conflict present between the plaintiff and any other single person. The nature of the lawsuit should be the deciding factor.

It always has been a matter of puzzlement how someone can sue a company for one's job after being fired. It would appear that one can sue for financial recompense but would not expect to be able to keep working at a job after winning such a lawsuit. The atmosphere surrounding such a case would appear to make it nonsensical for the person to want to stay. Whenever any employee decides to sue for his or her job, it is best for the company to try to make a financial settlement if it feels the person has a valid case. If the suit is between two employees, it is best to avoid involving the company itself, outside of trying to arrange for the two people to continue working in a productive, calm atmosphere.

2

AT HOME
IN THE OFFICE

AN OFFICE CAN fairly be described as a place where a group of people who have nothing much in common, and who will never see one another again after they leave, will be existing in the same proximity as two people who are married. It is conceivable that you will spend more time with your secretary or boss than with your kids, more time at the office than at home, and have more topics for conversation with co-workers than with your wife or husband.

This can be very unnerving. You may have little in common personally with your co-workers, yet you may spend most of your best energies joking and laughing with them. You may hate your ad salesman, but you will have to be more polite to him than to your mother-in-law. It's a wonder there are not more scratch marks on office walls.

The key to getting along in this situation is to approach it with prudence and good manners. This is what etiquette is for—to get along with strangers, people you don't know well or ultimately don't care about. The base point of etiquette for office interaction is to abstain most of the time. Do not let your hair down and tell all to your co-workers. Do not bare your soul, do not display all parts of your personality, do not tell them your hopes and dreams, plans and schemes.

Remember these things about the people you work with: They are there to make a living for themselves, not to provide an audience for your jokes, attitudes, personal habits, or hang-ups. Do not bore them. Do not interfere with their sensibilities. Try to make their lives as pleasant as you want them to make yours. The Golden Rule applies: Do unto others as you would have them do unto you. It has nothing to do with religion, but everything to do with getting through life safely.

Remember that a lot of people do not want to be at work at all. My editor at one of the magazines I worked for once said (actually, he said it a lot) that since you have to work at all you should try to make life in the office as pleasant as possible. His way was to arrange to have little surprise parties for people on the staff whenever their birthdays occurred. Whether it actually surprised anyone I don't know, since it happened to everyone, but the parties were fun and helped to make things better all the other days of the year.

It is this sort of attitude that is important: a genuine respect and consideration for the people you work with, based on kindness, without getting overly involved in one another's lives.

SPACES

Very few people have totally private space in an office situation. Even if you have a private office with a door that can be locked, it cannot be said that this is "your" office in a true sense. It is for your use as long as you are with the company, to provide a place for you to work in relation to other people. The fact that people must respect it as your space is a matter of etiquette, but you cannot truly view it as your home.

We all have to share work space. That is the nature of a company, of a working area. The only thing that endures there is the work itself; the workers are transitory. This situation leads to a host of special problems. People go on strike for better working conditions; people become irritated with certain other people they must share this temporary space with; a whole set of manners must be developed based on expediency, on getting the job done while not stepping on one another's toes—or at least coping with having toes stepped on.

It is never a good idea to view an office as being your own, even though you may decorate it and make it as personal a statement as you can. You may stay in it for twenty years, but from one hour to the next it can suddenly belong to someone else.

During the temporary time you will occupy your work space—be it six months or thirty years—it is important to try to make that space as pleasant as possible. The only thing to remember is this: Don't expend all your creative energies trying to get comfortable. When it comes to business etiquette, comfort and pleasantries must continually be kept in balance with creative fulfillment, financial remuneration, and your future career advancement.

OFFICE ROOMMATES

When dealing with shared office space the people actually "living" together must make their own decisions about the mundane procedures. They know best what they need to function in the space and they should make a point of discussing each other's requirements and deciding what compromises, if any, must be made. If they run into unsolvable conflicts, they can ask their immediate supervisor to arbitrate, but they should present a set of suggestions on which the final solution will be based.

One of the funniest problems of this type came up between two newspaper feature writers I knew who hated each other and had to share office space for a while. One was into design and decided that it was better architecturally to leave the overhead lights off and work only with desk lamps. The other could not see well enough in the dim light—since she was not near the window—to work at the typewriter.

Every morning she would come in and turn on the overhead lights. He would come in a little later and turn them off. Then they'd argue. He accused her of having a deficient sense of design. He eventually went to the boss and complained, and the boss refused to listen to his tales of woe. The deadlock was finally broken when one of them went to another company.

The problem was never actually resolved, since it involved a true clash of personalities and deliberate stepping on each other's toes. One would use the other's phone line to make business calls so his line would be left free for friends to call. One smoked continually, which drove the other mad. It went on and on, and there was no solution except to provide another office for one of them, which wasn't possible. The problem came about because two very talented, very smart people hated each other's guts and had no basis for a cooperative relationship. They were both right, and they were both wrong, because they couldn't come to a compromise and preferred to hate and grouse at each other.

IF YOU REALLY HATE EACH OTHER . . .

It happens that two people who come to hate each other must share space or constantly come in contact with each other. This is where maturity is called for. Life is not always adjustable to our petty needs, and two people who hate each other in an office have the easy option of not dealing with each other past the necessary interactions of business. It is acceptable for two enemies not to talk to each other, not to greet each other, to go about their work as if the other were not present. It is *not* acceptable to broadcast their particular dislikes to other people in the office. Hatred is sometimes a fact of life, but a running feud is not to be tolerated in an office. Keep your enmity silent. Formal politeness provides a tool for getting along without true interaction. Spitefulness and petty complaints must be avoided.

If an occasion ever arises to take a small step toward ending the enmity, it should be done. I knew two people who had offices across the aisle from each other for years and hated each other venomously. It was resolved when one of them returned from a business trip to a special place and brought back some highly desirable mementos to show the staff. He asked the secretary to choose one for herself and, on an impulse, told her to pick another one out for the enemy across the aisle. The secretary was startled, but took the offering across the aisle and placed it on the woman's desk, saying who sent it. A very happy "Thank you" came across over the partitions, answered by a warm "You're welcome," and the two became famous friends, doing favors for each other over the years that followed. It never hurts to let the barricades down no matter how bitter you may think you feel about someone.

The big block to compromise between two feuding co-workers is that they are probably enjoying the battle too much to give it up. They can focus on it, obtain endless anecdotes for cocktail parties, and bask in the knowledge that others are watching the show and enjoying it. It is as difficult to give up as some more positive achievement. If they stopped to think about it, they would realize that their hatred is often based on mutual respect.

If two people cannot come to a cease-fire, but their feud is not affecting their work or anyone else's, they should be left alone to settle their differences themselves. If work is affected, then an arbitrator must take action, whether or not the feuding parties ask for one. Whatever the arbitrator's decision, they must agree to accept it.

On their own they may find that there is someone with whom one of them can trade offices. My own opinion is that if two people in an office hate each other it is important to separate them. They should not expend useless efforts to try to cope with each other when it is plain that they will never succeed. An office is a place to work, not to get along with a mate. If their points of disagreement are based on personal clashes, and work is not involved or affected, they or their boss should try to reshuffle offices. If they cannot get along with anyone at all, then their employment should be made temporary until they pull their acts together.

ON THE RADIO

Things are done in offices these days that would have been inconceivable twenty, even ten, years ago. One of these is keeping a radio playing at one's desk during working hours. We recognize now that such things may help make the work more pleasant, so radios are tolerated. Any company that has an art department is familiar with the idea that a radio and work go hand in hand.

Music in the office is a nice touch, as long as it doesn't interfere with the work of the people who don't need music to work or who are disturbed by it. The Walkman radios solve the problem easily, but many people prefer music in the air, and conflict arises.

It is easy to say that the person playing the music is the one who must surrender when it comes to a showdown, but in fact the situation is more complicated. This is not a subway or a bus, after all; the person with the radio has a right to make his working conditions as pleasant as possible. Who decides? The people in the conflict should be made to come up with a compromise that will suit them both. It is not fair to place the burden on the boss, since any arbitrary decision will favor one over the other and lead to resentment. The boss should not have to take time out to settle such a dispute when the two persons involved know their own needs best.

A poll can be taken, of course, and if everyone wants music the radio can go on. If anyone objects, then it's on with the earphones. In offices where much of the business takes place over the phone, any unbusinesslike sound in the background should be avoided. Music in an office should be appropriate to the work being done there.

WHERE THERE'S SMOKE, THERE'S IRE

It seems incredible, if you think about it, that there are still people who insist on smoking in certain places. The evidence is in, as the saying goes, and the word is out. Smoking is detrimental to health; it's superobnoxious to many people who do not smoke; it's a clear fire hazard in certain areas. But still there are intelligent people who insist on lighting up, right there in front of the *No Fumar* sign.

It is, of course, bad manners to light up a cigarette in someone else's office without first asking if that person minds. It is an outright insult to walk into someone's office carrying a lit cigarette, cigar, or pipe. Many people object to the smell of a cigar or pipe, because the smoke is so distinctive that it can't be ignored. Some people *like* the smell of a good cigar; others find pipe tobaccos to be a pleasant addition to the air. But few people are neutral about them.

All smokers should be aware that their habit is something that cannot be ignored by anyone else in the room. Militant smokers take the position that when the smoke is no longer visible it is not there, thus placing themselves in the wrong from the start. Smoke pervades a large area very quickly, permeates clothing, invades the lungs of nonsmoking people in the room, and removes private choice immediately from nonsmokers.

We enter the area of etiquette here because the nonsmoker is placed in the position of either having to ask the smoker to put out the fire or having to stop the smoker from lighting up in the middle of the action—which is always an awkward thing to do. It's like stopping someone from telling a joke you've heard before—there's no graceful way to do it. The basic rule for any smoker is this: Never place someone in the position of having to ask you not to smoke. Always ask if the smoke will offend the nonsmoker before lighting up.

If the nonsmoker is truly irritated by smoke, he should say so when asked. There is no reason to have to fight for air to accommodate someone else's addiction. It is always bad manners to ask a nonoffender to adjust to an offender. It is worse manners to smoke defiantly; cigarette smoking is not such a fundamental right that it should lead to a militant defense of it. If a smoker cannot hold off for a brief time without lighting up, then there is a more serious problem here than nicotine addiction.

These things should be remembered by smokers and nonsmokers alike:

- The nonsmoker is not harming anyone's health by requesting to be spared the fumes of tobacco smoke.
- There are plenty of areas where the smoker can use tobacco freely and nonsmokers must exercise tolerance. One's own office is not such an area.

- If the nonsmoker is not truly bothered by the smoke, he or she should not make a fuss about it; both sides must exercise accommodation whenever possible.
- A smoker should not take it as a personal insult if asked to refrain from lighting up. Smoke is very irritating to many people. The nonsmoker should not be viewed as a nitpicking complainer if he says the smoke bothers him.
- It is bad manners to walk around with an unlit cigarette in your mouth or hand since it grabs the attention of people who wonder what you are about to do with it.

If you have a private office and you do not want people smoking there, you should make it clear to co-workers and take your chances on outsiders whom you must entertain in the office. Unless you have a health problem, it is not in the best of taste to ask guests to refrain from smoking unless they have the grace to ask if you mind. You can arrange your office so potential smokers are placed in a position where their smoke won't blow directly on you. If the smoke is surrounding your head and causing you discomfort, then tactfully ask the smoker to hold his cigarette in another position so the smoke doesn't get to you. If you really want to wage a polite war of nerves, equip the office with a small fan and let it blow the smoke somewhere else.

The rule of thumb about smoking is this: If you must endure it on a one-shot, short-term basis, let it pass. If you are working closely with a smoker, tell him or her that smoke bothers you and arrive at a compromise. You must be more frank with co-workers than with strangers, since you are, in a sense, sharing living space with them, and it would be absurd to expect a stranger to accommodate all of your desires.

If you work in an open office, you cannot reasonably expect smokers to refrain from smoking all during the workday. It is usually not even possible to segregate smokers from nonsmokers, since offices are set up to utilize space in a way that is efficient to office procedure. In these cases, nonsmokers are pretty much at the mercy of smokers, and since smokers are not noted for their mercy, you can either look for another job or make a complaint to the personnel people and let them figure out a solution.

Nonsmokers should do their best not to be offensive in expressing their resentment of smokers. Although too many smokers take the strange stance of defending "smokers' rights," which seem to come down to their right to disregard the rights of anyone else, the fact remains that they *do* have a right to smoke . . . in certain places.

If a person is smoking on an elevator with you, remember that the ride will not last long. The nonsmoker can take comfort in the knowledge that anyone who smokes on elevators these days ranks with the people who walk down the street with their radios blasting. You may politely request that the smoker extinguish his or her cigarette, but there is never any good reason to be rude in the way you approach the person. One smoker friend of ours got this from a stranger:

"Do you know how ridiculous you look standing there smoking that cigarette in an elevator?"

Our friend rightly answered, "Do you know how ridiculous you look with your stomach overhanging your belt?"

You see where rudeness can lead, even if you're in the right.

Fortunately for smokers, there are certain places in business where they can legitimately expect to be allowed to smoke without interference. One such place is in the reception area of a company. Some receptionists place signs asking that there be no smoking in their area, but this is a clear breach of etiquette and should not be permitted. The reasons are simple. Many of the people who wait in reception areas are nervous. They may be salesmen or people to be interviewed for a job, perhaps about to meet someone they have never seen before. They can reasonably be expected to be more nervous than normal, and if they are smokers, they will need to smoke. All reception areas—except those at offices of the American Cancer Foundation—should permit smoking and provide ashtrays. If the receptionist doesn't want to tolerate this, then she or he should request a different type of position.

DECOR AND RANCOR

It is natural to place one's personal touch on one's own little space in an office. Pictures of the kids, the wife, the husband, the rock star; mementos of celebrations and conventions; gifts from publicity agents—all help make an office a minihome. But some items are acceptable for office decor, others are not. Pictures, fun items, anything you choose should avoid the obscene, the leering, or the blatantly sex preferential. In shared spaces a full-length poster of Bo Derek doing whatever it is that makes her Bo Derek may run into some objections from the roommate.

Holidays bring out a desire to festoon the office in seasonal finery. Some people dislike Christmas decorations in an office; others love to garland and tinsel every available typewriter key, make color Xeroxes of red and green Santas, and do a whole host of pine-covered things. Non-Christians may object at times, but in such a case the objection would be considered rude. It is bad manners to expect someone not to celebrate a holiday simply because you don't share the observance. If two holidays of different religions occur, such as Hanukkah and Christmas, then decorations should commemorate both holidays. It is bad manners to observe one holiday and ignore the other in a mixed office.

NO NOSE IS GOOD NEWS

It is extremely difficult to maintain the "shutter" between your office life and your private life. When does a pleasant question about someone's weekend cross over into nosiness? Usually it depends on the person, but even a close office friend may not always step over that line without causing some embarrassment. It is most difficult to discuss some aspects of your private life without inviting questions about other parts of it. How much of what you do is to be considered intimate, how much is to be displayed?

There are certain questions, of course, which never should be asked, no matter how innocuous you may intend them to be. Generally these subjects revolve around marital status, income level, age, or where one hangs out socially.

Needless to say, there are questions that can be asked pertaining to all these subjects, and there are times when the information will be offered. But the ways and means of asking are what make the difference between good and bad manners, nosiness or valid interest. For example, one would never ask this question about someone's marital status:

"Why is a nice-looking guy [or gal] like you not married?"

It is within the bounds of etiquette to ask if a person is married or single, but it is not polite to probe further. The implication that everyone should be married unless there is a reason is rude to begin with; there may be some reason that is embarrassing to divulge to a stranger.

By the same token, it is all right to ask someone if he would like to talk about the reasons he is getting a divorce, if you are friendly enough to offer some comfort or helpful advice. Likewise, sharing some aspects of a problem such as your own divorce very often helps your co-workers cope with your mental pain during this difficult time. Since a divorce may affect one's work at an office, whereas being single does not, the etiquette is clearly defined.

It is considered very bad manners to ask a co-worker how much he or she makes, and even worse manners to tell how much you make. Personal income varies so much among personnel of equal position and job load that disclosure of income may cause repercussions. Some companies will reprimand or dismiss people for disclosing their salaries. The idea that an employer can pay whatever he likes to an employee, based on his evaluation, goes all the way back to biblical times and is never considered a matter for discussion.

Other areas of nondiscussion include asking someone how much she paid for something she is wearing, or asking someone else how much he spends on entertainment. Anything that is not volunteered on money matters is not to be asked.

Any personal question that asks "Why?" is bad manners. "Why do you wear your hair like that?" "Why don't you go on a diet?" "Why were you out yesterday?" Any question that exacts an explanation for an action is considered bad manners. Casual curiosity just for the sake of making conversation is also in bad taste and should be avoided. If you are bored, it's better to get a Rubik's Cube and focus on that.

AGED IN WOOD

Despite the fact that the Beatles, the Rolling Stones, and Sophia Loren all are over forty, it is still considered impolite to ask certain people how old they are. In some employment situations it may even be illegal. Someone who is obviously under twenty-five is not likely to object to telling his or her age, although many young male executives become surly if they think you think they're too young. Middle-aged women may not respond favorably if they think age is going to be discussed in their presence; some older men may be sensitive as they see their careers entering the twilight.

Discussions of age should not be conducted for the purpose of determining how old one person is. It is almost impossible to determine an age group that doesn't have some objection about being that particular age. You're either too young, too old, or just about to go over the hill. The emotional responses to pinpointing age are real enough to warrant treading carefully.

The same applies to weight. Our slim-conscious society makes it shameful in some people's eyes to be overweight. I heard a very tiny, petite woman once ask a health expert how much he thought she weighed. The man unthinkingly said, "One hundred twenty pounds." The woman turned bright red, the man then apologized, saying he really was not able to gauge weight on sight, and the woman, shattered, informed him that she weighed only 106 pounds.

Never ask people how old they think you are or how much they think you weigh unless you want a true answer. If you want flattery, don't expose yourself to truthful responses.

TONGUES THAT CLACK

The allure of gossip is undeniable. People love to talk about what others are doing, even if the others aren't doing much. There is a thrill in telling stories on others. Unfortunately, such tattling can lead to damage, outrage, or just plain hurt feelings. It is always best to avoid the temptation to gossip. If you do know something, you must judge seriously whether it comes under the heading of fair conversational topic or is gossip about a private affair that should not be passed around. There are certainly times when it is perfectly all right to talk about other people. If there weren't, we would live in a very quiet world. Even some amusing incidents of gossip are not necessarily taboo. The censorship is to be exercised on items that cause damage or hurt in some way, no matter how small.

It may happen that you become informed of something about a co-worker or someone in the office that you do not need to know. This can sometimes happen without intention on your part, but most frequently it happens because someone is desperate to let everyone else know. Whatever information you receive, it's best to let it stop with you. If the information can help you advance your career, then you know what is the best course of action. If it is simple gossip that is no one's business but the people it is about, ignore it.

Grapevines in the office are funny things. They usually carry bunches of gossip that are useless to anyone. For example, in a large nonprofit organization it became common knowledge that the head of the organization was going to go on to another company. The change was not to be announced immediately, since the vacancy wasn't to occur for three months. It leaked, and everyone in the office who could possibly be considered for the position began discussing why he or she was the most qualified to step up into the head position.

It became ludicrous as each of them jockeyed for meetings and lunches with board members to discuss something that could not even be mentioned outright. By implying that you are available for such a position you admit that you act on the basis of office gossip and therefore are possibly not qualified for a top position; on the other hand, you want to be considered for it.

The best course of action in such a case is to go to someone outside the company who has influence with someone inside the company and have that person find out what you can do to make yourself available by popular request. I knew one woman who even went so far as to leak the news to a business publication to provide a valid opening for her to apply for the job.

Many things are fair in business that would not be tolerable in "real" life. The general point to remember is that gossip has almost no useful aspects in the business world. If you are a truly valuable professional, you won't have to rely on the office grapevine to know what important events are happening in your company; you'll be among the first to be informed.

THE YENTAS

Out of the goodness of their hearts—to soothe and satisfy their egos—there are people who (a) have to know everybody's business and (b) try to do something about it. These are the meddlers who rush forth, leading with the shoulder, offering a comforting attitude, and hoping for every juicy, thrilling morsel. They only want to help. And they should be told to stay out of it.

People going through emotional stress of any kind will usually talk to any openly sympathetic listener, whether or not that person is someone they would normally have much to do with. The rule is to be careful in your times of stress not to become attached to a yenta. When the period of stress is over, you may not want to be friends.

Many meddlers provide comfort only because it feeds their egos to be needed, especially in times of delicate stress. They generally will fuel as many fires as they put out, since they love the drama that plays and soak up depression and misery like some sort of super paper towel. It's best not to allow such people to become overly involved, in your affairs, whether personal or business. It can be dangerous to your career to have such persons know too much about your problems, since yentas not only soak up information but squeeze it out as well.

On the other side of the coin, there are people whose lives are a constant series of melodramatic events, who go from one tragedy to another, whether romantically or socially or professionally. Something is always wrong, and they will talk about it endlessly. They also try to involve you in their affairs, since they enjoy the performance and reprise of their crises so much. If you are fortunate enough to have a yenta to pair with this kind of person, then you have a match made in heaven. If not, steer an even course past them, and never let on that you have so much as a headache. If they ask, a formal, polite smile as you head off in another direction is all that's needed.

STRANGERS IN THE OFFICE
Politeness to Temps

In any office one finds that the secretary becomes ill at times and a temporary typist is called in to fulfill some of the duties. This person is not fair game for your charms or your curiosity. Usually these are people who either do not want anything to do with office life or are trying to raise some money for extras like food and rent while they wait for a break somewhere else. In any event, they probably have something better to do with their time than get to know you. The best thing to do is leave them alone, past a perfunctory greeting, unless you have some work that they are paid to do.

A pleasant, businesslike approach is the best policy here. If you are looking for another secretary and this person might conceivably fill the post, then a little more friendliness may be acceptable. But in general strangers are usually in an office only for a brief time, and usually the reasons for their presence are to do business with someone. Unless they are rifling someone's desk, the best policy is to leave them alone as much as possible.

Mysterious Stranger

If a person is standing confused in the middle of the office, it would be not only rude but absurd for no one to offer help. To go up to someone, however, who does not concern you and say, suspiciously, "May I help you?" is rude. If you suspect someone should not be there, ask the receptionist to verify it first. People doing business in an office should not have to be cross-examined by anyone who feels self-important in the halls. Nor should they have to explain their presence to people they will not be doing business with.

Escorting Guests

When a man is visiting a woman at her office, he must allow himself to be escorted. This is her turf and she is the hosting party. She may open doors and let him go first, defer to him as a guest, and all of it is correct good manners. This is especially true on the man's first visit; he does not know his way through the corridors and it is more convenient to let the woman handle everything.

This etiquette holds no matter what the sex or age of the people involved: the host always escorts the guest, unless the guest is so familiar and so regular a figure at the office that the etiquette can be readapted without confusion.

Guests should always be escorted by someone—an assistant, a secretary, or the host—from the reception area to the inner destination. After a first meeting the guest should also be escorted back to the reception area or the elevator by the host. Regular guests need not be escorted if they know the office plan well and can be trusted not to make side trips into other offices.

It is considered bad manners to one's co-workers to allow a guest to wander unescorted through the office area. As an unknown person, he may cause suspicion or apprehension among some of the staff.

Who Stays?

If you are already in someone's office for any reason and someone else comes to the door seeking entry, it is up to the hosting party to ask you to leave in favor of the other person or to stay. You may bow out yourself if you must leave, but do not make the assumption that the host automatically wants you to go.

It becomes a matter of embarrassment for some people who find themselves in the boss's office when another high-ranking exec comes in. The first visitor is trapped in an uncomfortable position. There is no reason for this. High-ranking execs are as subject to good manners as anyone else; just because they appear in the office does not mean they must preempt someone of lower position.

In this case, the host should ask the first visitor to step out for a while; or the high-ranking visitor should ask if he can interrupt for a moment, or request the host to contact him as soon as possible. The lower-ranking visitor should never be placed in the awkward position of having to perch uncomfortably, wondering whether to go or to stay. The confused visitor can say, "Shall I come back later?" but it is best to let the other two take the initiative.

It may happen, on the other hand, that the first guest may need to take a break, and this can be used as an opportunity to do so. Just say, "Excuse me, since you are here, I can use the time to check on something at my desk," then head for the water fountain or wherever you want to go.

BRATS AND CATS

People do bring their children and even their pets to the office at times. It is a practice that should be avoided unless there is no other alternative. It is difficult to imagine many cases when one would have to bring a cat to the office, but a midday veterinarian's visit may be one acceptable reason. One high-ranking woman executive of an insurance firm received a call at the office from the manager of her cooperative apartment house informing her that her dog was screaming in the apartment. The animal's mate had had to be put away over the weekend, and the dog was unable to cope with being "abandoned" during the workday. The woman had to taxi home, get the dog, and taxi back to the office, where the dog wouldn't get off her lap. Eventually she had to farm out the animal to her family, but it was a case where the dog had to be either brought to the office or tranquilized.

It is not rude to bring a child to the office, but it is an interference if the child cannot be controlled properly. Single mothers or fathers may at times find it necessary to have their children at the office. If possible, the parent should try to take the day off from work instead. Although children are often a delight in the office, a parent should remember that someone's workday will be disrupted by the child's presence. An animal, in fact, is less likely to be disruptive, unless someone decides to play with it. Children are inquisitive, they do not understand the concept of work well enough to remain quiet, and there is usually no place for them here.

LE SALON

It is definitely out of line to entertain friends socially in the office. Even supercasual offices are not geared for an influx of buddies socializing. It is all right for someone to pick you up at the office for lunch or for a date after work, but it is not acceptable to allow friends to stop in during the workday to visit. If you have your own office and want to have someone in for lunch and you know the outer offices are usually empty during this time, it is all right to do so.

By the same token, it is rudeness in the extreme to drop in on someone unannounced at his office and have the receptionist call through. If someone does this, the best approach is to tell the receptionist that you are in a meeting and aren't available. Then later inform the offender politely that you cannot accommodate such visits.

We were told a story by a computer-company executive who received a visit from a friend of a cousin who was in the same business. The visitor showed up at the reception area and the unwilling host allowed him to come in. The man started to talk very loudly about personal affairs, and the host said, "Excuse me," got up, closed the door, and told the guest that his remarks were uncalled for and it was not acceptable to visit people at business unannounced. He then thanked the visitor for contacting him, wished him well in finding work, and escorted him to the elevators.

CHOOSE YOUR SCHMOOZE

In many offices there are people who are frustrated something-elses. We were told of one advertising salesman who was a song-and-dance man in his youth and who had never quite forsaken the wicked stage. He carried it around with him and spent much of his free time in other offices telling his stories, singing the old songs, and generally interfering with work. Once someone suggested he come back at a better time, and the man blew up and left in a snit. The person who had made the suggestion decided it was better to have him in a snit and staying away than to have him well disposed and reviving "Good News" next to the secretary's desk, so he let it rest.

Schmoozers, singers, kibitzers, and friendly types should be asked to save their recitals for the company picnic or the convention in Jamaica. They have limited use for breaks in the office. If these intramural troupers will not accept the cancellation notice, then someone in authority should ban them from the offices where they do not do business.

TO TALK IS TO LIVE

It happens that many people in offices can get all their work done and still have a lot of time to talk. At times you may find that you have become the confidant of a co-worker you would not normally choose to be close to and are being used as a shoulder to lean on. The unwanted talker tells you all the details of his or her marriage and family, and kids' school problems. Some of these types tell you the most intimate details of their sad love lives. It really becomes tedious trying to get any work done while these people take up so much of your time.

The only approach is to be totally frank and say you have work to do and can't talk. If you want the relationship to die out totally, just always "be busy" when the person looks in. It is very bad manners to subject co-workers to accounts of personal problems unless the parties are already close friends. In that case, the problems can be discussed at a time convenient for both talker and listener.

EARLY TO BED/ LATE TO WORK

Some people can't really adjust to the nine-to-five schedule no matter how many years they work. My favorite story is about the chronically late man who never got to work before ten thirty any day the whole eleven years he worked for a company. Everyone helped him maintain the fiction that no one important was aware of his lateness.

Each morning he arrived, scooted—skulked, rather—from the elevators into the mailroom, and deposited his coat there. He'd roll up his sleeves, loosen his tie, and breeze past the office of the president looking somewhat as if he'd been working all morning. Because he was so good at his job and so well liked by everyone, no one ever betrayed his "secret."

Many late arrivers do cause inconvenience to others in the office, though. For many people, chronic tardiness is not the lovable character trait it was with the man above. Usually lateness is inconsiderate since people must delay their own schedules if there are meetings and a key person is late; people who are prompt generally resent the fact that a co-worker is late.

If someone's lateness or early departures do cause problems for you, it is polite to ask the person to lunch and discuss the way the situation is affecting your work. Then give him or her a chance to change. If you meet with rudeness or no action, then you are within your rights to make a complaint. These complaints are fair inasmuch as the boss may need them before being able to take an action or to have a basis for a reprimand.

LAZYBONES

The same etiquette holds when one of your co-workers is a chronic goof-off and your own work load is increased because of it. In this case, fairness to yourself and to your boss takes precedence over good manners and minding your own business. It becomes your business if your work is affected. A complaint of this sort is a business action, not a stab in the back.

THE COVER-UP

The question of when to cover for a co-worker may come up in an office. Someone may need to take extra time at lunch and ask you to cover for him. Someone may be having problems at home and be under so much pressure that he needs some help. There is a time to respect a person's temporary inability to produce at work, and there is a time to protect your own energies when someone's lack of integrity causes a drain on your own working efficiency. If someone is an out-and-out goof-off or manipulator on the job, there is no real reason to extend the benefit of the doubt. Make a formal complaint and let your superior handle it. If you know the person and are aware that he or she has a problem, offer to listen and try to help arrive at a solution that serves both of you well. There is nothing wrong with accommodating a good co-worker during temporary times of stress. It is when they become permanent patterns that you must demand a change.

No co-worker should expect his colleagues to cover for him as far as screening phone calls or dealing with out-of-office problems, however. A separated spouse who calls, creditors dunning for payment—none of these should be the concern of your co-workers. If you do not want to talk to someone on the phone, just tell him to call you at home or, if you are being harassed, take some legal action or make a complaint to an official agency.

COVERING FOR THE BOSS

Not all bosses, surprisingly enough, are competent in their jobs. Very often they depend heavily on the talent of their staff to make them look good. There is nothing wrong with this as long as the staff people are properly paid and credited. A boss is not necessarily as good as the people he or she holds together.

The problem arises when the boss's incompetence endangers careers and interferes with productivity. In this case the staff is faced with the unattractive prospect of covering for the man who can fire them, or banding together to dump him—something that is so improbable that it is not even worth considering. If the boss is incompetent but well disposed toward his staff, then it is worth covering for him. Up to a point. If his superiors come to one or several members of the staff to verify suspicions of his incompetence, then a true picture should be presented.

THE BOSS'S JOB

If you are in the position of being offered your boss's job, you may be ambivalent about taking it. If you feel you can do the job, you should accept it. If the offer is more a feeler to see if you might be available, you should discreetly make it clear that you would be, even if you are not sure. Do not ever present doubts about your ability to high-level people in the company. Keep them to yourself.

Many people in such a position will defer to their boss even when the boss is incompetent in many ways. One should defer only when one is convinced he or she does not want the job under any circumstances or if one is absolutely sure of the boss's mutual loyalty. If it ever comes to light to a scapegoat-making boss that you were offered his position and refused, he will try to get rid of you anyway, simply because the company considers you able to replace him.

It is an extremely secure person who will groom someone to take over his own job. Most people prefer to groom people who are unable to take over the job, as a form of self-protection. The rule about protecting bosses is that such loyalty must be a two-way street. It is useless to protect someone who will throw you to the wolves at the first sign of trouble.

THE SCAPEGOAT

It happens in many companies, maybe all of them, that an upheaval takes place, based on a lack of productivity or a bad economic climate, and the ax begins to fall, making a wide sweep. At such times the people who have positions of influence begin to protect themselves by passing blame on down the line to whomever they can hand it to. The buck never seems to stop anywhere; blame is passed from hand to hand like a hot potato.

These times are upsetting, especially if you find yourself placed in the position of being a scapegoat. It is especially difficult when there is no real blame but the company becomes a victim of a bad economy.

There are people who make the use of a scapegoat an integral part of their career survival kit. When the going gets a little rough, a person like this will immediately start setting up someone for the kill by discrediting him or her so that when the time comes—if the time comes—the lamb is properly prepared for the sacrifice. I know of one particularly adept survivor who always has at least three scapegoats prepared to fire every few months just in case he needs to. In the meantime he lulls them into a false sense of security by assuring them that he relies on them, while discrediting them to the company owners. It works very well, actually.

This practice is very cruel and underhanded, especially since there is no real defense against it unless you also want to use your creative energies to become embroiled in a banana-republic-style game of musical chairs. The only "polite" thing to do in these types of situations is to keep looking. Never remove your name from the active list of your employment agency; always keep your ears and eyes open for new jobs; make lots of friends in high places. And hope for the best deal when the time comes.

BOWING OUT GRACEFULLY

It sounds negative and defeatist, but it is not likely that a scapegoat has much chance of turning the tables and being vindicated. You are working from a weakly defensive point, since you have been discredited already. To make an attempt to save yourself would expose you to contempt, despite the fact that you are in the right.

The best approach is to get another position lined up, then get the best severance deal you can. You are in a good position to do this, because the person sacrificing you is working from guilt and will try to overcompensate by being generous with severance pay and benefits. If he realizes you will be cooperative and not cause a lot of noise and upset, he will also cooperate in getting you money. I'm always amazed at how many times scapegoats are kept on retainer as advisers to the companies that have fired them.

As a scapegoat it is best not to bad-mouth anyone unnecessarily (although if you do in this case, you will not lose any image credibility, since everyone is emotionally on your side). The more generous and professional your behavior during this time, the better you will look in the long run. Although nobody will come to your rescue, your long-range renaissance is better protected if you maintain an air of grace and self-control through the difficulty. Every career has high and low points; if you can accept this as part of living, your overall career will be kept at a higher level.

I knew one scapegoat maker who called his scapegoat the day after firing him and complained because everyone in the office was "in a brown funk" about the situation. The scapegoat spent a half hour trying to make his ex-boss feel better.

BACK STABBERS

Co-workers may also try to do one another in, sometimes out of sheer malice, at other times to inprove their own positions. At times a co-worker may pose as a friend and secretly be helping the boss, who is looking for a scapegoat. If a co-worker is acting alone to stab you in the back, it is necessary to fight back by confronting the back stabber. If you have any information to fight back with, then use it directly instead of warning the person with it. No quarter should be given to a back-stabbing co-worker. A strong demand to bring him out in the open and expose his underhandedness is required. If a direct confrontation and warning to desist do not work, then ask your superior to take disciplinary action against your enemy.

Many years ago, before things became as liberal as they are now, I knew of a man, very talented, married and with two infant sons, who almost became the victim of a back stabber. The enemy began telling people in the office that he had proof that this man was homosexual. In those days the accusation (which was false in this case) was as good as the truth, since people reacted strongly to this type of thing. The accused man suffered agonies wondering how to fight it, since the matter was handled by innuendo and insinuation. It turned out that the accuser was trying to push him out of the job because his talent showed up the back stabber. It was brought out in the open when the accused took the matter to his boss and demanded that something be done. Fortunately, the boss was fair, and the back stabber was told to find another place to work.

FIGHTS IN THE OFFICE

Although arguments in the office are not uncommon, actual outbreaks of violence involving the use of fists, such as hitting each other or actual brawling, are extremely rare. There is really no reason to tolerate this kind of behavior, and the participants should be put on some sort of disciplinary suspension or fired. This drastic move is necessary because of the psychology involved: once the taboo against striking a co-worker has been broken, such conduct is no longer unthinkable and can happen again.

Yelling arguments in the office are also extremely upsetting to the people who see or hear them. They leave people wondering what to do. If two people are fighting and the fight lasts briefly, then it will, of course, set off a blaze of gossip until everyone knows what happened. It is necessary after any outburst for the person in authority to question each participant and make sure that peace has been restored and cooperation is still possible. No drastic measures need to be taken except to make it clear that there are acceptable ways to overcome differences and making a loud scene is not one of them.

If the fighting becomes a regular part of any one person's approach to business, he should be required to determine if psychological help is required; if he refuses, his employment should be made contingent on his making a change in his behavior.

If two people are arguing, only their superior should try to interfere. If the argument goes on and on, they should be forced to call a truce. If actual violence occurs, several people should try to stop them.

ARBITRATION

It is the mark of a true professional that he or she need not run to the boss over every little office upset like a kid playing in a sandbox. It is not the job of a boss to deal with runny noses, personal squabbles, and dislikes of his staff, or to arbitrate petty feuds. In the first place, it is bad form to bring petty enmities into the office or to allow any situation to reach the point of fighting. Arguments based on real professional disagreements are valid, but they should never reach the point of becoming personal antagonisms.

Matters in the area of personal likes and dislikes should be brought to the boss for arbitration when they actually affect one's working situation. If someone chain-smokes and you can't handle it, the boss can be asked to mediate. If someone has a personal problem that disrupts the others he works with, it is the kind of thing that should be turned over to your immediate superior for resolution. If someone is sick, dirty, argumentative, loud, or disruptive, the boss cannot be left out of it.

If you have a co-worker who shares space with you or if you depend on someone else's output to do your job well and that person is not doing the job, then you can do two things. First, you can discuss it with the person himself. If you do not see any immediate change, then you are duty-bound to the company as well as to yourself to take the matter to the boss. It is not wrong to do this; it is only proper business procedure. Many people feel guilty about doing such a thing, and most people do not like to do it just because of personal feelings about such actions. It is never wrong to insist on a reasonable working situation that provides an atmosphere for you to function in. It is not bad manners to insist that a slacker be forced either to produce or to leave when his behavior affects your own performance on the job.

KING CRAB

There are certain positions in life where you can be as crabby as you like and it won't affect the people around you. There aren't many; the only one that comes immediately to mind is that of obituary writer on a newspaper. And the only one I knew was a pretty friendly guy. Perhaps he heard something every day of his life that made him glad to be alive.

People who are moody, depressed, or generally unpleasant can affect the moods—and in some cases the work patterns—of other people in the office. It is not fair to bring your moodiness to the office. People do not feel comfortable approaching someone who is in a bad mood. As a result they may put off asking about things related to work until the weather is a little more clear, and delays in decisions and productivity may result. You should never ask the people you work with to put up with your moods unless they occur infrequently. If you find yourself in a negative frame of mind, then you should try to keep it to yourself, or at least make it clear that you do not expect anyone to wait it out or deal with it in the office.

If these moods are caused by something in the office, then you should discuss the problem with your boss or with personnel to see if you can arrive at a change in the conditions that are causing the problem. If the problem is from outside the office, then you are duty-bound not to lay it on your fellow workers.

WHEN ANGER WORKS

Although it is never polite to use anyone as a target of anger or to blow up just to let off steam, there are times when exasperating situations call for firm action. One designer who owns his own company says, "Much as you may hate it, the only thing that is left to you at times is to get ticked off, bring out the big guns, and let people know you are angry."

Because of the decay of service in business today, these situations become more and more common. The designer I quoted generally tries to maintain a polite margin the first few times, but when he gets no results, he tries this tack:

"Look, I've asked you politely for weeks and there are still no results. Why are you forcing me to be a heavy? I don't enjoy hassling people or shouting. We have a job to do; there's an enormous amount of money involved. Why do I have to get down to shouting and threats to get a job done?"

Very often people who perform services in business find they must take care of the ones who make the most noise before getting around to the softies. It is for you to decide whether it is worth the constant hassle to deal with these people, or whether you should find someone who can do the job for you the way you prefer.

There are people who tire of having to scream for service and stop screaming. They quietly cancel and move on to other suppliers. There are not many people who relish the role of being a son of a bitch; if they have to play that role more than they feel is tolerable, they take steps away from the situation.

Yes, there are people who love to be the heavy, shouting and making threats. It gives them a sense of their own importance to tear through people's emotions. But they are not the majority, and they will make a fuss even if one need not be made.

There is a way to be polite but firm and still get results. It takes a while to establish this with clients, and it usually involves some hard-nosed business practices, such as adding interest to bills for delays, or demanding better prices on subsequent orders. The best policy is always to have a backup competitor and make it clear to suppliers that after a reasonable delay the order will be withdrawn and business taken somewhere else. By following through, with a polite expression of regret that you cannot accommodate them, you will establish yourself as the prime person to be serviced, and your soft words will carry more of a cutting edge.

FREEBIES

It's amazing how many people will crowd around you when you're the one whose desk catches the freebies. For several years I was the one, and since the freebies were usually things I couldn't use, the word got around. The man who headed the mailroom would come in every Christmas to collect his pound of cologne, and during the year he would ask outright what was in the package from Aramis, the envelope from Canoe, the large box from my mother. It was the Great Unspoken: I wanted my mail to get out of New York; he wanted some to land on his desk. A friend of mine nicknamed him Evita.

In general, it is rude to ask someone to share his freebies; on the other hand, it is unfair for one person to profit greedily on something that is due to his position at a company. Some companies have a policy about freebies: they go into a common pot and everyone gets their turn at them. *Esquire* magazine used to store them and have a rummage sale every year where employees could pick up some very nice bargains. I believe the proceeds went to some worthwhile party for the staff, but everyone benefited.

Gifts will be sent out as part of regular business, and no one loses and everyone can gain. *Cosmopolitan* magazine has a good policy of rotating free trips as they come in among the staff. In any event, freebies, unless they are actual personal gifts to a particular member of a staff—such as a bottle of fine cognac sent as a thank-you from a company to someone—are fairly shared among the staff. The reason for this is that everyone in a company is doing the job that attracted the freebies. The person to whom they're addressed only represents the company being courted.

Discounts are something else again. There are always situations where someone, because of his job, has access to discounts from a corporation that may make, say, stereo components. It is definitely a breach of etiquette to ask for these discounts for other members of the staff. The discount is made available not to the whole company but as a courtesy to the person who is in contact with the manufacturer. It is *only* a courtesy, and to extend it past that person would be an imposition, and a costly one. Since the courtesy was extended to gain goodwill from the contact person, it should not be assumed to be an invitation to pillage and loot. It takes too much in the way of paperwork and delivery and man-hours to ask for discounts for all. It is also discourteous for a person to overuse the privilege. Perhaps orders of one of each product would be all right, but never do your Christmas shopping this way unless specifically invited to do so.

It should also be remembered that the person who is the contact for the freebies and discounts is a person who has a job to do for the company, and he or she should not be viewed as a shipping agent. It takes a lot of time and hassle to order things in this special way, to get the money collected, and to see that the product received is the right one and one that actually works properly. The same state of affairs exists on the other end—the person who works for the manufacturer of the discount items. He has more to do than spend hours getting out products as a favor to some stranger who works with his contact. At this point, the goodwill that the discount offer was meant to engender becomes an imposition and disgust takes the place of goodwill. The contact person loses his clout and your company no longer commands any respect.

PETTY CASH

Someone always manages petty-cash disbursements. It is necessary to respect this person's time, since he or she is usually con-
scientious enough to have a pretty well organized schedule. Anyone who is responsible for petty cash should set up a time of day
regularly to handle anyone who has a voucher, instead of allowing
people to come up at random and interrupt work. It is not the business of petty cash to bail out someone who is short of lunch money.
Anyone who lays out cash for the company in small amounts can
certainly take the time to make sure he or she has enough in case
the petty-cash person is busy.

LOANS

There is much lending of lunch money, cigarette money, and pin
money among office employees. It is all right to take advantage of
this once in a while when you missed your chance to get to the
bank, but it is a real imposition to mess up someone else's budget
regularly by borrowing, then repaying, small sums. This constant
going in and out of someone's cash is obnoxious and rude. You
should get advice about your personal budget if you are always
running short, or you should do without the purchase you want to
make rather than have someone support you in this way.

One person was always borrowing from me in small amounts.
One day I realized that he had owed me about ten dollars off and
on for months. I went to him, asked for my money point-blank, and
refused to give him another loan. It made no difference in the
friendship, but it made me better able to cope with it.

If you borrow from anyone, it is your responsibility to remember
the loan. Write it down in your engagement calendar and pay it
back promptly. Often people forget they gave you the money.
When they remember sometime in the far future, they find it difficult to bring the subject up.

GETTING MONEY BACK

If someone does owe you money and you want it, the best thing to do is ask for it straightforwardly. You can say, "Do you have the money you owe me yet?"

If he does not, then you can ask when he will have it. It is best to set a limit on time whenever lending money instead of letting it go open-ended. It is not rude to do this, nor is it rude to ask for your money when you want it.

THE PERENNIAL BUMMER

It is bad manners to continually borrow or "bum" things that cost money, such as cigarettes, candy, or any other item. Cigarette bummers are probably the worst offenders, Because it seems mean to refuse to give someone a single cigarette, many people do it but resent it. It is not only the idea of the money and supporting some-one else's habit; it is the bother of having to reach in and provide the cigarette every time the bummer comes by.

Some solutions may be to offer to lend the person the money to buy a whole pack; to join with other borrowees and make a produc-tion of buying him a pack with the stipulation that he buy his own from then on; or to refuse point-blank to lend any more, and refuse to discuss it further.

3

STYLES AND
SENSIBILITIES

PERSONAL IMAGE IS extremely important in the office. You should develop a positive sense of style that is in line with the image you want to present and that fits in with the people who work with you in the office or do business with you outside.

Mannerisms are the things people notice and react to. The way we move, talk, dress, the colognes we wear or the ones we don't, the personal noises we make and the general atmosphere we engender are all part of the package that people use to decide if they like us or loathe us, want to work with us or hope we find another job escorting ocean liners around Cape Horn.

In today's society there is no excuse for bad grooming, bad manners, bad presentation. We know too much; we are all educated and we all have easy access to the products and services we need to make ourselves appealing to society. If you work in an office you are choosing to be with people constantly, and you must consider their sensibilities in reacting to you on a personal level.

65

PIGGISH BEHAVIOR

There are certain types of behavior that are inexcusable in any-one, anywhere. In general, these aspects of human behavior are concerned with the passing of wind, as it used to be called, or doing anything that reminds one of the scatological function, involves scratching oneself in the private parts, spitting in the street, belch-ing regularly and loudly, picking one's nose, sucking one's teeth loudly after eating, eating loudly at table—in short, anything that refers to the animal function in ways that may tend to turn your co-workers' stomachs.

The worst "pig" story I ever heard was about the office manager who sat on people's desks while talking to them. Once, after dis-cussing her assignments with one very well bred young woman in the office, the manager lifted one leg, expelled a loud burst of air from his person, and went off into his office, leaving his staff in shock. He was also in the habit of spitting on the sidewalk while walking with them, and making loud noises while he ate. Some people, it seems, never get over the fun they had while living in the college dorm.

Part of the etiquette problem here is that most people are psy-chologically unable to tell the offensive person that his or her piggy behavior is out of line. They should be told, especially in cases of extreme rudeness, such as belching and farting in the office. Some behavior, such as nervous scratching, may not be incentive to make such a united front, although it may be helpful to suggest profes-sional help if you know of any.

In any case of obnoxious personal habits, it is all right to tell the person discreetly that some of his habits are getting to you and ask him to desist. If it keeps up, you have the option to ask that you be moved to a part of the office away from the person. Remember that not all people are offended by the same things; someone else, not as sensitive, may not object to a knuckle-popper at the next table.

Some of the things that people do find objectionable are these: belching; farting; spitting; nose picking; tooth picking with fingers;

making noises to suck things out of teeth; scratching private parts or buttocks; reaching into clothes to adjust underclothes, such as bra straps or stockings; knuckle popping; beard picking or scratching; scalp scratching; pipe sucking; tapping teeth with fingernails; fingernail filing and clipping; fingernail chewing; cuticle munching; boot grasping while legs are crossed; humming; whistling; noises made with air through teeth; rustling fingers up and down on nylon fabric or walls; chewing hard objects such as pens and pencils; chewing soft objects such as neckties and scarves and hair ends; twisting and playing with hair while conversing; gum "games" such as popping or rolling the wad in the mouth; chewing a dead cigar or cigarette; eating candy while talking to someone. The list goes on. I know of one person, totally polite, who kept a series of hair-strand sculptures on his desk that he had fashioned during periods of lull in the office. And he demonstrated the technique proudly.

Not all these habits are necessarily piggish behavior. Such a judgment rests in the eye of the beholder. But all these things are somehow related to hygiene and, as such, are not appropriate for public display.

Boorish behavior also indicates an inner hostility and anger, and its expression, coming as it does in the same form a dog might use when locked in the basement, does not suit someone who has aspirations to the respect and admiration that go with business success.

It is never appropriate to perform grooming chores in the view of your co-workers. If you want to use the electric shaver, close the door or go to the men's room. Women are the greatest offenders in public grooming. The desk is not the place to fix your makeup or get ready to meet the lunch crowd. Nail care is best done at home or in private. I never came across a company that did not provide adequate space in the women's lounge to perform whatever beauty operations were adequate for the day. It is not good to do them in the office.

Men are the worst offenders with nail clippers. The noise sets many people's teeth on edge, and the practice should be avoided. Gum chewing is a childish-looking habit and is considered "dirty" by some people. Never talk to anyone with gum in your mouth. It is also rude to talk to people while smoking, but this particular form of bad manners is so commonplace that the people who voice objections are the ones who receive the attack. It is not polite to force your addictions on other people, nor to object when they ask to be spared.

NEW STYLES/ OLD STYLES

The requirements for business wear and grooming seem to have changed drastically over the past twenty years but the truth is that the only real changes have been in the cut of the clothes. Conservative companies still have rigid dress codes for their employees. Dark suits and ties are still the basic uniform for men; some companies still require women to wear dresses or outfits that include skirts rather than pants.

Men are still being asked by some employers when they intend to remove their beards, the implication being that one's employment status is darkened by facial hair. That many companies do not care if their people show up in denims and T-shirts or Balenciaga revivals as long as they do the job does not mean that this attitude is at all widespread. People in the fields of publishing, commercial art, and entertainment areas are extended almost total freedom in choosing what they will wear to work. People in the other nonuniformed professions are extended what might be called an inch of leeway in dress and hairstyle, but a strictly limited code is expected to be adhered to.

From an etiquette point of view there is no doubt that certain companies have a right to expect a certain level of uniformity in dress and appearance. Others do not. It all depends on whether or not the company's profits are affected by the way its people look.

SETTING THE STYLE

Top executives are responsible for setting the company image. In some cases written guidelines are actually presented to new employees prior to or at the start of employment. Although it is not up to the top people to go around personally to each employee every week to see if he or she is toeing the line, it is important that the boss convey the expected behavior to the staff.

Dress codes are important to most companies. In the past fifteen or more years, all dress codes have loosened up, although with the renaissance of conservatism people are opting for more formal clothing as a matter of choice and fashion. It is not important what the code is as long as it is reasonable and flexible enough to be followed.

Companies which deal in elegance and fashion through their products—such as cosmetics and fashion industries—are right to expect their employees, all the way down to the receptionists, to dress in the height of fashion—and even to wear makeup. Charles Revson once required his female employees to wear the maxiskirt during the time it was supposed to be in fashion (but wasn't catching on). Because of the nature of his company, he was within his rights to do this. A company that made bathing suits, on the other hand, would not be making a reasonable dress code if it followed his lead.

Some company heads feel that it is not necessary to have written guidelines for dress, etiquette, or employee behavior. They expect people to adopt the company style through observation and imitation. It is best, however, to set forth some sort of code of expected behavior for employees to take confusion out of the matter. If they know what is expected, they will find it easy to follow and expand on the general guidelines.

At this point in time dress codes should be limited to rules that prohibit the wearing of patently unsuitable clothes to work, such as revealing, provocative, or outright sexy articles of clothing. If a person's job requires that he meet many outsiders and represent the company out of the office, it is reasonable to expect him or her to dress up. Even if in-office attire is casual to the point of Levi's and T-shirts, appropriate clothes must be worn when going out to meet people in a business capacity.

If an employee who is not at the executive level is creating a problem regarding dress or behavior, then the solution should be handled by the personnel department or the employee's immediate supervisor. In the case of a *wunderkind* making a shambles of the corporate image, the matter should be taken up with him or her at the executive level. Usually, if the person is supertalented and there is a desire to keep him or her in the company, a compromise or adjustment should be made, even if it means that certain diplomatic duties of the offender should be reassigned to someone who talks and dresses a little more according to the norm. One finds that the highly individual clothing of supertalented young people is often willingly put aside if the occasion demands it. Such people usually enjoy the spotlight after their concession to conventional behavior.

There is, in fact, more of a desire to accomplish something in business among today's young generation, and less of a desire to go against the grain. It's almost as if they wish to spend as much time as possible using their talent to produce and don't want to get sidetracked by issues that impede advancement. As long as the company does not try to interfere with their private lives, they are willing to go with the code during the workday. They like money, this new breed, and are more willing to go along with the rules to get it.

THE TABOOS

There are certain things that a boss may not say to an employee politely; there are times when an employee must go through hierarchical channels to communicate something to a high-level executive. Bosses may not make snide remarks about an associate's appearance, tiredness, or any highly personal matters. If an associate's way of dressing is offensive or detrimental to the company image, then the matter is to be broached on that basis. An employer may not say, "What's wrong with your skin?" unless the person is asking for a reference to a dermatologist.

If the associate does indulge in careless grooming habits that make him or her look foolish to others in business, a boss who has a good relationship with the person may offer advice in a discreet way. I knew of one talented young legal administrator who was raised as the son of a diplomat. Somehow his education had left out the importance of daily brushing as a preventive of tooth decay. Because the plaque on his teeth was noticeable to tooth-conscious Americans, his supervisor took him aside and explained that it was important from several points of view to brush regularly and see a dentist twice a year. Then he gave him the name of a dentist. The man was young enough at the time to accept the advice, and he later thanked the adviser for it since it turned out his teeth were on the verge of surrendering.

If a person has discolored teeth, it would not be appropriate for the boss to mention it, since such a condition has various causes, some of which are the result of nature. The boss must use discretion and take each situation as it comes. Or leave each situation as it stands.

It is equally inappropriate for employees to tell bosses what's wrong with them. Such matters are only to be broached when the employee's personal image has already been attacked and he or she feels the boss has overstepped the boundaries of business.

In the opinion of many successful people, the higher you rise in business the more important it is to have a reliable confidant who tells you when you're slipping in matters of etiquette, grooming, or whatever. A good secretary/ boss relationship can be the answer, but one also needs someone like an associate executive to whisper in one's ear at times. The woman executive who arrived at an executive sales meeting one morning and was unaware that her silk blouse had become undone under her suit would certainly want to be notified rather than sit through a whole morning watching other executives avert their eyes. A close colleague can whisper the fact and the woman can excuse herself and rearrange the outfit.

The most embarrassing story I know is of the superelegant woman executive, who was also a member of European royalty, working in a high-fashion business in New York. She came out of the women's room one day, walked down the hall, through the reception area, and down another hall, past open offices, with her high-fashion skirt caught in her panty-hose waistband, revealing more of her legs than was fashionable. The wide-eyed executives, secretaries, and receptionist looked on in horror and silence until the receptionist thought to call the woman's secretary and tell her the problem.

It would have been very inappropriate to stop the woman in the hall and tell her that her dress was hiked up. She could not very well have fixed it in front of everyone. In cases like this, it is less embarrassing to let the person get to a private place first, then let her or him have the news and get over the embarrassment if there is any.

It is also best to remember that one is always among adults, who presumably are aware of the fact that under each business suit or dress is a human body. Only schoolchildren will act silly and poke fun. Buttons and zippers are not so reliable that we should allow them to cause us devastation when they don't cooperate. Fix the problem and don't dwell on embarrassment. Everyone has fingers and toes, after all.

ROSEANN ROSEANNADANNA

It is always a matter of consternation when someone you report to is discovered in a state of disarray. Your boss may be sitting there, seriously discussing an important subject, and you are watching a droplet hanging from somewhere inside his nose as he talks and nods. Or your boss sits and you see a flash of shirttail where his fly is open. Or your boss, a dignified, stylish woman, has some romaine lettuce stuck to a tooth, or some egg on her chin.

Don't act like you're gonna die! And don't say, "Hey, boss! What are you tryin' to do—make me sick?" Lean forward with a smile and say quietly that the person has a problem that he or she is not aware of. If the fly is open and you are also a man, you can say so directly. If you are a woman and you think it may be embarrassing, you can wait it out, then pass the information on to another man to go in and tell him; or you can excuse yourself and write a fast note to him, saying, "I'm sorry, but your pants are open, and I thought it would be easier for you to correct the matter if I were not with you. Call me back as soon as you wish."

It is a tricky situation. Some men would not be embarrassed and would, in an adult way, zip up and continue as if nothing had happened—which is the truth. You must suit the action to the person.

There is no reason not to inform your boss when some situation like this exists. It is worse to allow someone to go through the day with egg on his or her face. If the person is superdignified or in some august position, it is best to pass the information on to his or her assistant or secretary and let that person deal with it.

SCENTSIBILITY

In any place where there are people thrown in close, not necessarily voluntary contact with each other, personal hygiene is a duty. All the TV ads come true in an office, because you are working arm in arm with many people who are not family and not emotionally committed to you.

Personal odors due to lack of hygiene are inexcusable in America today. There are enough varieties of soaps, deodorants, and laundromats to keep oneself clean without any unusual outlay of cash. No one should be forced to sit and deal with unpleasant personal odors that can be handled by simple grooming.

We heard once of an executive who did have a strong, unpleasant body odor that was due to his own metabolism. In this case, there was no solution, and he was open about it, so people were willing to accommodate him. But dirtiness is not acceptable, and the boss or personnel department should take steps to demand that the offending party wash up or ship out.

YOUR TWO SCENTS

An office is not a place for definitive colognes, pervasive perfumes, distinctive hair sprays, supersexy clothes, advanced nudity, or bare feet. A cologne can be annoying to people if they have their attention caught by it often during the day. A strong cologne is like a loud noise or a sloppy display visually.

Many people do not consider that colognes or perfumes may be offensive, since the primary reason for using them is to please the senses. For the office, personal scents and fragrances should be kept light, pleasant, and nondistinctive. They should be noticeable only to someone who is standing very close to you. Your cologne should not be powerful enough to reach the nose of the person at the next desk. Highly distinctive or noticeable scents should be reserved for social occasions. If you are near someone who does wear a fragrance that is too much for you to ignore, it is reasonable to ask him or her to tone it down. Some scents only have an impact on initial meeting, and the nose quickly tunes them out. Others may constantly jolt you during the workday and become as irritating as gum popping.

Since fragrance is not a bodily produced scent, it is not necessary to think of offending someone by asking her or him to relieve you of it. It is a simple matter to say that the particular fragrance affects your sinuses in a bad way and ask the person to try something else for the office.

It is not rude to wear a cologne to the office, however. One never knows what the reaction to any cologne will be, since some fragrances cause allergic reactions in some people but not in others; some may love a certain scent, while others become repulsed by it.

MR. BAGGY PANTS

When I did jury duty it was a joke among us jurors to watch the prosecuting attorney's suit fall into shambles before our eyes day by day. He wore the same suit all through the trial. On Monday it was pressed neatly. By Friday it was a rumpled mess. It was like watching Pigpen in "Peanuts," and it cut into the attorney's effectiveness because we developed a real distaste for that suit. A month after the trial I saw the lawyer at the theater. He was wearing the same suit, and I automatically looked down to check the day of the week by the bagginess of his trousers.

People are always writing to Ann Landers about how to tell their boss that he shouldn't come to work with his lapel held together with a safety pin, that his clothes should be dry-cleaned, that his shoes should be resoled. But no one ever seems to take the direct route—telling the person himself. It is difficult to do, but it is good manners to tell someone you like that he is hurting his image by his grooming practices.

KNOWING THE CODES

In any company clothes are very much a part of your job, and if you delude yourself into thinking that people don't notice, then you are hurting yourself. I once had to go on a tour of a company set up specially for writers. When I got to the meeting place, one guest was saying to another. "I see you decided to opt for casual clothes today, Sam." Since the man was in a suit and tie, he obviously had not thought about the fact that corduroy was less than correct for an occasion that was somewhat formal—that of representing your company as a guest of another company.

Sam was greeted with embarrassment by the publicity man, who expressed it only through a red face; but he drew an irritated glare from one high-level executive who came to greet and host us at lunch in the company dining room. Sam could not apologize, of course, for his clothes; the only thing was to accept his mistake and not make it again. It is bad manners not to make yourself conversant with the acceptable dress requirements for certain situations. It was considered an affront to the company hosting Sam for him to show up thoughtlessly suited. In the office and for many less stilted occasions, his garb would have been more than acceptable. For a "state" occasion such as this, more fastidiousness was needed.

Inappropriateness of dress is, therefore, as offensive to people in certain business situations as ripped or soiled clothes. It gives them something "off" to deal with in a situation that may already be tense in some way, and that little detail becomes the one thing they let themselves focus on to be uptight about. I have seen a group of businessmen at lunchtime walking in a group where one of them was dressed in a light blue leisure suit, while the rest wore dark business suits and ties. They were going to great lengths to avoid talking to him; he looked awkward and could not have been a comfortable part of the group. He probably did his career some harm by not being aware of what was the expected image.

Not many people have the freedom to dress the way they want in the office and still forge ahead. Even the most rebellious person finds that he has to dress like other people at some point in business. The thing to do in these cases is to wear your sensible "free" clothes whenever you can, and make it clear that you will dress appropriately when the occasion demands it.

DON'T MENTION IT

If you find yourself in a situation where you are not appropriately dressed, don't talk about or try to refer to it obliquely by way of apology. The only correct thing is for everyone to ignore it and focus on the business at hand. If the occasion is purely diplomatic, of course, and formal attire is being worn by everyone except you, then you must not remain at the affair. To wear informal clothes to a formal event is a blatant gaffe, and you must not stay. Dressy or strictly formal occasions require a certain decorum that cannot be broken, since the reason for the affair is as formal as the attire. It is equally foolish to wear formal clothes to a nonformal occasion, although it is not necesary to leave if you are overdressed. You can in this case say that you were mistaken and thought the occasion was formal.

Do not refer to any personal grooming problem or aberration at a business meeting unless someone asks. Never apologize for the way you look; just try to look good. If you are growing a beard and are at the scruffy stage, do not bring attention to the fact that you are growing a beard, as a sort of apology. If someone says, "Good luck with your beard," you can smile and say, "Thanks."

It is rude to bring up another person's skin problems, bitten nails, or anything similar. The only time one mentions someone else's grooming habits is in a complimentary way.

SEXY CLOTHING

I once worked with a young woman, about nineteen, who was especially nice looking. One day in the summer she showed up in sandals and a very light cotton sunsuit with a bare midriff. It ended the workday for many of us because she was so sexy we couldn't think of anything except how not to look at her while getting a real good look at her. She was such a sweetheart that no one made any sleazy remarks or passes, but her clothes were inappropriate for the office. At a lawn party she wouldn't have been so spectacular, as a matter of fact, since the suit was not tight-fitting nor even that revealing; but it was extremely sexy in a context where it didn't belong. Her husband must have told her, since she wore it only once. Because of her naiveté, a kind, confidential explanation from her boss would have been appropriate.

Whether it's cologne or clothes, sexiness in the office should be muted. Some people would be sexy in an elephant blanket, of course, but an office is a place to dress with decorum, in clothes that do not purposely take the focus away from the business at hand.

Women in business do not always follow appropriate guidelines. I knew one secretary who used to wear a low-cut black cocktail dress to work. Some women in summer, to fight the heat, tend to reveal more skin than is appropriate for business. In this matter the commonly accepted apparel of your company is the guideline. In general terms, women should dress in nonsexy, conservative wearables, without sacrificing style, color, or self-enhancement. Dressing well at the office, but not revealingly, is the best rule of thumb.

Certain height-of-fashion or fad-type clothes may or may not be appropriate to wear to the office. If you work for a record company, it would not be unseemly to get together a punk look for the office or to dye your hair magenta. If you work for a medical supply firm, such distinctive fashion may be a turn-off for the people you deal with.

The way you wear your clothes and keep them pressed and clean displays your good manners and your consideration for the other people who work with you. The five senses must be respected in a business office, even if you don't do it anywhere else. Any assault, visual, audio, nasal, or tactile, should be avoided.

REPAIRS

Every company should provide access to needles and a variety of colored threads so that employees may make, or have made, repairs to torn clothing during the workday. There are few things as debilitating as having to go through part of the day with a sweater tied around your waist because your pants ripped out in the seat as you stepped out of the cab that morning. It is also to the company's advantage to provide brushes, an iron and board, and some special spot removers in case someone gets splashed on the way in to work or spills food on himself at lunch. Accidents are unavoidable, but repair kits can save an important day.

It is up to the individual to keep extra shoelaces, combs, grooming supplies, socks, or nylons on hand in case they are needed. Repairs can be made in a lounge, in an empty office, or in one's own office.

HELLO/ GOOD-BYE

When one works in a company for a long time, one may get into the habit of not greeting or saying good-bye to co-workers every day. It is not considered rude to abstain from the constant greetings, since people can become irritated with the same sprightly "Good morning!" chirping at them each day. But it is also not necessary to be so formal with the people you see on that basis five days a week. These greetings are always nice, but it is not rude to leave them out at times.

COMPLIMENTS

Pleasantries, compliments, and expressions of concern are always polite. It would be depressing to work in a place where nobody ever observed the little politenesses that are really noises of affection. All animals need them, even if they are clichés. They take the place of stroking and they soften the experience of being thrown into close, intimate quarters with strangers.

Compliments in an office situation should be made only when they are sincerely meant: for the woman who has a new haircut or looks particularly nice, or the man who has worn a complete suit for a change. Do not, however, go up to the secretary who has worked there for years and suddenly say, "You have beautiful blue eyes." It is a personal, semiromantic compliment and not appropriate. It is appropriate to say, "Your hair looks very good like that," if she has just changed the color or had it restyled . . . but only if you mean it.

Compliments in an office should be used sparingly, sincerely, and only when something outstanding on a personal level has been achieved.

FLATTERERS

There are many unpleasant names that are used for the process of currying favor with those above. Terms such as "brownnosing" or "sucking up to the boss" describe acts of sycophancy which people find offensive. In fact it is despicable to try to get ahead by using tactics of this sort, and it is never good manners to indulge in a despicable act.

The best approach when you are faced with a sycophant is to pass him or her over. It is usually an indication of real incompetence if a person must resort to such means of getting ahead. It is an insult to the person receiving the attention, and an insult to the people who are doing their jobs seriously, to allow this sort of thing to continue.

If you happen to have a boss who is susceptible to such flattery—and there are bosses who expect it—the best course of action is either to roll over the boss if possible or to look for employment in a more realistic atmosphere. I did know of one superegotistical man who had regular coffee-klatch meetings early each morning. He would then extol his previous day's and evening's triumphs for his employees' admiration, and expect everyone to make some sort of murmur of pride over him. He lasted a long time, unfortunately, but many talented people under him did not—which ultimately hurt the company he worked for.

One way to handle sycophancy is to make it known to the boss that the other members of the staff do not like to contend with such actions when they are striving to do their jobs. Another way is to freeze out the sycophant from any interaction with his colleagues in the office. In most offices it is impossible for anyone to buck his co-workers. If he does not have the working cooperation of the rest of the staff, he cannot do his job. Since a sycophant doesn't want to do it anyway, he should be shown the consequences.

GLEEM!

Smiles that are false, or used as part of a friendly image, can be irritating to people as well as embarrassing. Some people are not aware that they use smiles falsely, but doing so, as well as punctuating sentences with laughter to somehow soften any possibility of being taken the wrong way, is to be avoided.

In business, you definitely can be fully dressed without a smile if it is not come by naturally. When greeting an applicant for a job, a smile is a good way to put him or her at ease. But constant smiles that become strictures of the mouth discourage people from communicating with you.

A general rule is to greet any stranger in a business situation with a friendly smile, and otherwise to reserve smiles for times when they just happen naturally. Or for times when you aren't in a real good mood but don't want people to feel you are angry with them.

THE LANGUAGE OF ETIQUETTE

Besides the commonly used foul words one should avoid coarseness of rhetoric as well in a business situation. This is not the use of four-letter words, but the vulgarization of language: words such as "Hi" instead of "Hello"; "Sure" instead of "Of course"; and a host of others. Much of this comes from a desire to be superfriendly, but that approach is not correct in business. It is better to be politely friendly and still maintain a certain formality of language in certain situations.

Receptionists, especially, must be made aware that certain stiff-sounding expressions actually sound very good to a stranger's ear. They add elegance to the company image and indicate that the company is willing to take the extra effort and time required to observe the formalities of respect when addressing clients and business associates.

It would certainly sound very bad to a caller to hear a person say "Yeah" instead of "Yes"; "Sure" instead of "Surely"; "Wait a sec" instead of "Will you please wait?" Just as one must be careful to use the words "Please" and "Thank you" when dealing with one's everyday co-workers, it is useful to cultivate one's tongue above the high-school level when addressing associates in more formalized business situations.

Diction also has a subtle psychological effect that can make people judge us well or badly in business. If one has a heavy regional accent that makes one difficult to understand in some areas of the country, then steps should be taken to shed some of the heavier overlays. Here we run into a matter of preference, of course. Some people may find a heavy southern accent up North to be totally charming and useful. A Brooklynite may find himself or herself at a disadvantage in Boston if the accent is identified with certain old TV movies. One must choose whether to make use of such an accent or try to change it, depending on the reactions of business associates.

GUTTER TONGUES

What used to be called foul language is so much in evidence these days, particularly in what used to be called mixed company, that it seems almost prudish to bring it up at this late date. No matter how many times we hear Jill Clayburgh use the "F" word on the big screen, or how many times we hear cute little third-grade girls use Richard Pryor's favorite word, the senses are still jolted when someone cusses in the middle of a business chat. There is nothing pleasant about hearing intelligent people rely on the gutter for their vocabulary.

It is rude to use what we still call four-letter words in any business context. If you're tough, you don't have to prove it by falling back on the "F" word, the "D" word, the "S" word, or the "M." Fortunately, people still have an inhibition about using the "P" word, so all is not yet lost. The American vernacular is a colorful and useful tool, unmatched by any other language. It is only good manners to give it a shot. The American vulgar tongue, however, is limited, gross, and entirely too graphic for high-level use.

DIRTY JOKES

Dirty jokes are usually those that center on some of the grosser aspects of the sexual act and the mystique surrounding it. These days it is considered somewhat ridiculous to abstain from telling dirty jokes when most of our public conveyances have the same stories spray-painted all over them; but if we don't try to keep a high level somewhere, the whole quality of life will disappear.

Dirty jokes, offensive jokes, any jokes must be used judiciously. Even a "clean" joke may be offensive just because people become exasperated when they are forced into a laughing situation when they don't feel in the mood for it. Before telling any joke of any stripe make sure your audience is receptive.

THAT'S NOT FUNNY

People who would never think of insulting someone outright may actually do it on a regular basis by being what they think is funny around the office. There have always been jokes about certain significant ethnic traits, types, stereotypes, and in recent years these have taken a new tack to include put-downs of women, gay people, popes, God, Jesus, Mary, and Joseph, Miss Piggy, cripples, the handicapped, the blind, and especially the black.

There is currently a group of highly paid, highly placed Wall Street lawyers and executives who have formed a joke network. They spend much of their time thinking up outrageous jokes about anyone who is not a white, male Wall Streeter. Anything goes, no matter how gross, cruel, or vicious.

Without getting into the psychological roots of the matter, the basic question comes down to what kind of response you will get when you tell these jokes, and who will be offended by them. Needless to say, a joke about kinky hair will not get a surefire laugh from your black secretary, even if she's pretty sure of your true feelings. A similar joke about Italians, on the other hand, may get a positive response from Dominic in the mailroom.

When sailing into the area of ethnic jokes, you have to be sure that the people hearing the jokes will not be offended. This is not easy to gauge and you must take stock of your audience before cutting loose. There are things to remember around the office in the first place:

- It is a place to work, not to try out new comedy material.
- You should try to limit your joke audience to groups of one or two people to minimize the possibility of offending someone.
- Never tell an ethnic joke to a person of that ethnic group

unless you are absolutely sure of the reception you will get. Some people like to hear jokes about their own ethnic background; others get real mad.

- Never tell a black joke to a black person unless you are also a black person. Because of the real prejudice that has gone before, you are most likely to meet with embarrassment or anger as a response, not appreciation or laughter.
- Don't continually tell, say, Polish jokes to a Polish person just because he or she may have thought they were funny at first. After a while they begin to irritate through boredom, and the person may begin to wonder why you are always telling them.
- Don't become pious about ethnic humor. It is as rude to cut a person off in the middle of a story as it is to tell a pope joke at the monsignor's birthday party. I once started telling an Alitalia joke to a fellow Italian-American and she cut me short, twisted her face into a frown, and launched into a long, tedious reprimand about believing in One World and One People and how everyone is the same as everyone else, and if I wanted to tell the joke, I should tell it about "any" airline. . . .

Whether or not ethnic humor should be funny is something we must leave to Heaven. The fact that some jokes are funny to the people whom they are about is undeniable. It is reasonable to think that one member of an ethnic group can tell a joke about that group to a fellow member. It is not bad manners to laugh at yourself.

Although an office should never be seen as a tryout place for new comics, everyone appreciates the fact that jokes, humor, and funny stories, kept in proportion to the overall purpose of doing business, are not only acceptable but desirable.

PUT-DOWNS

In any relationship that is fed by relentless interaction the danger of falling into the trap of sarcasm becomes increased. Married couples, who may actually love each other tenderly, sometimes get into the habit of debasing each other verbally as a running joke until the put-downs become genuine. This can also happen in the office, where boredom makes people develop low-grade hostilities for each other anyway.

It is very rude to make deprecating remarks even in jest. The human brain, being what it is, will first take the put-down seriously, then immediately overlay the judgment of a joke. When you run into that person who doesn't go past the first part of the process, you end up with someone who's mad at you. It is essential in an office to maintain a strict judgment of every situation. If you're in doubt, do without when it comes to making a negative remark about someone, even when intending it as a friendly joke.

I once watched a very high-strung young woman become a bitter enemy of a co-worker who said that he didn't think a certain newspaper columnist appealed to a very discriminating audience. Since the young woman had just been saying she thought the columnist was amusing that Sunday, she took his remark as implying that she was stupid. The poor man was caught in a blazing retort for something he didn't even know he had done, and the woman stopped talking to him for years, even though they worked directly across the aisle from each other. You can't be too careful. The woman overreacted, but his unthinking remark struck a nerve.

WHAT'S YOUR NAME?

Names are superimportant to us. Unfortunately, it is easy to forget names or to mispronounce them. It is always good manners to try to get names firmly matched with faces and to ask for correct pronunciation from the source. It is good manners for an executive to know the names of all the people who work for him. Sometimes the company is so large that it isn't really feasible, but one should try to get as many names memorized as possible.

I once watched an owner of a small company ask an out-of-office messenger where someone's office was. The messenger happened to know, and the president asked this person, who did not work for him, to tell the employee to call him in his office. When the boy informed him that he did not work there, the president said, "Oh," thought a moment, then asked if he knew who could pass the message along.

Names are the last thing anyone should forget or not know within a company.

BAD SEEDS

There are some people with whom you can never get along. They are determined to be negative, nasty, and depressed, despite the compliments, help, and kind treatment they may receive. We had two of these bad seeds at different times. One was just plain incorrigible. He would not complete a task; then he'd lie about it. He would claim he had done it right and the copy editor was trying to "screw" him. He would order expensive books from publishers as "review copies" (we never reviewed books) and take them home. I saw him reading a beautiful book on da Vinci once and asked where he'd bought it. He said the publisher had sent it to him as a gift. Later, after he was fired—taking his pelf with him—the publisher called and asked if we would return the loaned copy and when we were planning to run the review. The departed employee had requested it on that basis.

Yet another bad seed actually was extremely talented and one of the best editors we ever had on staff. One day after work I went out and told him that we were very happy with his work and he was one of the best young editors I had ever encountered. He mumbled some self-deprecating remark, which I took as modesty. I pressed it: I said, "No, no, we are really so happy with you that I think you should know it."

He turned on me like a wounded animal and said bitterly, "I know what I can and can't do and I don't like people complimenting me just to make me feel good!"

I was surprised, since up to that point he had seemed a happy, cheerful person. I turned to look into my editor's office, but he just lifted his shoulders to say, "Don't ask me." I just said quietly, "Well, I hope someday you realize that you are very good."

I had made an enemy, and he still snubs me on the street. He is senior editor now for a fine magazine, and one of his coeditors had lunch with me one day and said, "He's a great editor, but no one can get anywhere near him to say hello."

You never know what psychological or emotional problems are visited on people. When they are young, these problems are covered over with the exuberance of youth. Later they become set if no help is sought. If the people are talented, they are able to keep their jobs and their co-workers just learn to cope with them. If not, they find it impossible to stay anywhere very long. There is no way to deal with them, politely or on their own negative terms. The best thing to do is give them the work and the space to do it and let them suffer alone.

THE HANDSHAKE

The most established form of etiquette in our society is the handshake. It is absolutely an insult to refuse to shake hands with someone, especially in a business situation. Even if your right hand is broken or not shakable for some physcial reason, you must offer your other hand, with an apology for not being able to perform the proper amenity.

There was a time when it was proper to wait for a woman to offer her hand to respect her preference. Now it is expected that both people will automatically put forth their hands together. It is not rude to forget to offer one's hand, but it is definitely bad manners not to accept a hand that is offered. Even business rivals are expected to perform this small courtesy with each other as an acknowledgment that our common humanity is more important than money.

If you are the type that uses touch as part of your way of relating, then make sure you do it formally and with respect for the other person. You should never put your arm around a co-worker's neck, even when you're friends, in an office situation. It is not appropriate. Save your displays of affection for later and content yourself with a smile, considerate behavior, a handshake, and pleasantness.

THE KISS

We will detail kisses and the times for acceptable kissing in chapter 5, "When Cupid Gets Stupid." The only thing to be said here about it is that kissing is still shaded with romanticism in our society and is not yet a fully accepted business amenity. It is perhaps rude to refuse a kiss offered in a business situation, but it is even more rude to offer one to anybody not considered a friend. You should offer a kiss only to someone who will be flattered to receive it as a platonic statement of friendship or to established friends in business.

THE "AIR KISS"

This established social mannerism takes the form of two people offering first one cheek, then the other, and kissing the air next to each side of the face. It is a European—primarily French—custom that is gaining ground as a useful tool in certain American business/social situations. It is a sign of true friendship when used in France since it allows you to honor someone with a kiss without implying any intimacy past mutual respect. In most situations it enables colleagues to set the tone for superficial, quick interactions without seeming brusque.

This "kiss" can be used to greet a great variety of people, whether close associates or just acquaintances. Because it is such a stylized mannerism one must be selective when using it. The recipient must have the foreknowledge that you are going to follow through with the air kiss, or it can fudge into a clumsy moment of embarrassment. An American, posed with a face coming toward his with the lips puckered, will assume you are asking for a kiss on the mouth or a single kiss on the cheek. When you instead launch past to kiss the air next to his cheek, then back off and approach the other side, there may be a clash of eyeglass frames somewhere in the middle, and a lot of confusion.

When "conducting" the air kiss with a neophyte, you should guide the person as if he were a dance partner. Use your right hand to guide his right hand, as in a handshake, and place your left hand on his right shoulder. Then guide him into the right posturings. And hope for the best.

WORKING WITH HANDICAPS

People who are handicapped in any physical way do not present any problems unless they or someone else around is uptight about it. Some handicapped people do use their afflictions as an excuse for bad behavior or to make excessive demands. Some other people become embarrassed around people who are handicapped and either can't get past the fact or try to compensate by joking about it. Some people do not take their handicaps as seriously as the rest of us and love to make self-jokes, not as a compensation but because they think they are funny.

The etiquette is to take the lead from the person with the handicap. If he ignores it, then so can you. If he makes a big fuss over it, he should be told that past special ramps and similar constructions, he must work under the same conditions as anyone else.

It is polite to help someone in a wheelchair get around when there is difficulty; it is polite to take on the job of helping anyone who needs or asks for help if it makes things easier. Many handicapped people live with physical pain on a daily basis. This should be remembered when dealing with them. The normal considerate and respectful interaction you would show any co-worker is required here. Don't change your personality for a handicapped person or treat him as being crippled other than physically.

Handicapped people, too, are bound by rules of etiquette. I once watched a man in a wheelchair insist on blocking an entrance to a restaurant that didn't have a ramp. The management offered to help pull his wheelchair up the single step that would take him into the restaurant, but the man insisted on calling the police because of the law that said restaurants in that state had to provide ramps.

REPEAT THAT, PLEASE?

I have known two people who were highly successful in business, made lots of money, and were never unemployed for more than a few weeks between jobs, and whom I couldn't understand to save my life because of their thick foreign accents. I was amazed to learn that both of them worked in sales, and most of their work was conducted over the telephone.

I became friendly with both of them, by chance, and I spoke candidly to one about the matter. I couldn't ask the other one because I still can't understand a word she says. The one who spoke said that he does become upset when people ask him to repeat things because of his accent, since to his own ears he speaks well enough to be understood. Nonetheless, I still ask him to repeat when I can't catch the gist of things, and he still looks annoyed. But at least we communicate.

If anyone has a speech pattern that is hard to follow for any reason, it is better to ask the person to repeat himself rather than take a chance on getting the information wrong. It is somewhat tiring having to strain to catch a person's words, and people who are able to improve their diction should do so even if it means spending some money for help.

The woman who is dearest to me has the softest voice in the world, yet is a successful vice-president of a large corporation. I am always politely asking her to speak up. Speech discrepancies do not, obviously, cut into anyone's career, but they can make things harder for everyone else.

A woman, highly successful in the more diplomatic areas of business dealings, once told me that her assistant would call me about a matter we were involved in. Before hanging up, she said, "Oh, by the way, Greta's from Sweden, and she has a thick accent. The only way to handle it is to keep asking her to repeat what she's saying." A foreign accent is not a mortal sin. In business it is best to get clear information, not to worry about asking for repeated information. If someone's accent is heavy enough, he or she is used to this and usually doesn't object.

IT'S IN THE CARDS
Thank-You Notes

The idea of sending a written thank-you note for anything has pretty much passed out of use in American society. Only the most fastidiously well mannered people do it today. Nonetheless, it is still bad manners not to send thank-you notes for gifts, favors, and special entertainments.

The thank-you note card itself can be either a foldover card or a flat card, with either an embossed or colored border, or plain. When using the foldover, do not write anything on the cover. Open the card and write your complete message inside. Sign your full name and company name.

Thank-you notes are not necessary for business lunches. They should be sent to companies that send you Christmas gifts or provide you with freebies throughout the year. Yes, it is rude not to acknowledge bottles of liquor, sets of cologne, and flowers that come in at holidays. The reason is not so much to thank as to let the people know that their gift has been duly received and appreciated. They need to know that the gift has not gone astray: it is important to them that you have received it, even if you think it is a crass, cold play for favors. A gift from a company must be treated with the same courtesy as a gift from a friend.

Always remember that in business a thank-you note is almost always the perfect and appropriate way to express gratitude for anything. Expensive thank-you gifts, such as lavish lunches or dinners that include fifty-dollar bottles of wine, are considered tasteless these days even by those who receive them. If your company deals in some way with expensive champagne, then a bottle of it as a gift is acceptable. Seldom is it right to spend a large sum of money on such things as gifts, especially in times of tight money. It makes you seem extravagant, and people do not like to do business with people who appear to spend money foolishly on useless items. Most people want their thanks in proportion to the favor. Never forget that the favor may have been done to cultivate goodwill.

Whenever it is necessary to pay special thanks to someone in a business context, it is better to send the thanks via a note or card. Thanks for favors, help, or special occasions should not be made by a phone call. A special thank-you is best exemplified by a special effort, and it is not considered much effort to place a call. Anyone who tries to use the phone on a business day might disagree, but there you have it. Also, a phone call can be interrupted or rushed or be made at a bad time, whereas written notes can be read at leisure.

It is always good to evaluate when a thank-you is required from you. I have always been vexed by people who send thank-you notes after you have taken them to lunch to thank them for something. It can go on *ad infinitum,* the two of you thanking each other into the cosmos. If someone thanks you for anything, it is enough to say, "You are welcome" or "Prego" or "De nada" or a host of other translations. A thank-you note does not require an acknowledgment.

It is a delight, however, to see elegant food manners in action. I have on several occasions had to entertain people at lunch or with drinks to interview them for stories I was working on. Clearly they were doing me a favor. It has always been a nice thing to get a note or call from them, not so much thanking me for lunch as expressing their pleasure at being able to join me. It is flattering in a nice way, and makes one feel less as if one has imposed on them and more as if they enjoyed being quoted.

Other Notes

When a woman marries and decides to adopt her husband's name professionally, she should send announcements to that effect to people who regularly do business with her. If there is a professional newsletter or publication in her field, she should also inform it of the change.

It is only necessary to send notes of congratulations on a wedding if you do business regularly with the newlywed person. No gift is required unless you have been invited to the wedding.

Condolences about a death in the family are always good manners, but not always necessary. If a co-worker has a death in the family, it is an occasion for group condolences, and even a gift of flowers if the company pays for it. Verbal condolences among co-workers can be avoided if a note is sent. It is often awkward for a person to speak condolences to a grieving co-worker, and a card is the best way to handle it. It also shows that you took some care to extend your sympathy.

Birthday wishes are always spoken; otherwise, the birthday is ignored. The reason for this is that in business one cannot be expected to carry on a subsocial life as well. Birthdays are personal. If co-workers want to give a card or take you to lunch, that's fine, but not at all necessary. The best tack about co-workers' birthdays is not to go past the basic greeting. Anything more may obligate a person until the office becomes a round of parties.

Business Calling Cards

Another aspect of business that is to be found only at certain levels is the use of a business card. People pretty much come and go in a business sense strictly on their own recognizance these days, without having to present a card bearing a name and company logo to back them up.

If you are in the kind of business that requires you to visit clients and associates frequently at their offices, it is good manners to present your card when you arrive. The card is also useful to leave with receptionists, to send through the mails with letters, and to leave as a remembrance in places where you wish to make an impression.

The card should carry this information:

- your name, as the focal point of the card
- the company name, or, if you work on your own, your professional appellation
- your telephone number or numbers
- your company or professional address

When you arrive at a new client's office, it is good manners to shake hands first, then at the next immediate convenient moment, place your card on his or her desk or the nearest table surface. It need not be picked up immediately, but it should be acknowledged with a thank-you. If the host places his card on the table before you do, it is a request that you do the same. If you do not have a card, thank him for his and take it and place it in your case or in your pocket or address book. Because so many people do not have business cards, it will not seem odd if you do not present one; but it is in the best etiquette to do so when visiting a business associate.

These cards are handy, as we mentioned above, when introducing yourself by mail. Always clip one to the upper left-hand corner of your letter, or insert it into the folded letter, so the person receiving it will have a convenient record of you. Most executives do not keep letters on their desk, but a business card can be kept handy, or taped onto a Rollodex card.

Illness Takes Its Toll

I heard it said that anyone who has hepatitis is sure to lose his job eventually. This is not strictly true, but the effects of the illness can be so debilitating that the victim may find he or she is unable to perform on the job well enough to continue in it. Any physical debility that occurs, whether it is illness-related or functional, may change one's ability to work so drastically that termination of employment is the only solution.

Many years ago we had a wonderful woman who was our managing editor and whom we all loved. She was near retirement age. One day I was talking to her with another person and she suddenly looked up at the lights, mumbled something, stiffened her whole body like a board, and shot back, headfirst, out of her chair and onto the floor.

By the time I got to the other side of the desk, she was grinding her teeth, and her tiny, retirement-age arms were quivering and tensed hard as a rock. It was low blood sugar, simple as that. And it happened again and again. She refused to eat properly, and we never knew when she would crack her little silver-stranded head open, at work or on a subway.

Somehow personnel managed to persuade her to go on sick leave until her retirement date, but she was so mad that she never spoke to many of us again. It had to be done, even if it was done with love. A business office is a place for business. It is not reasonable to expect a whole group of people to take care of you, or put up with your illness in the office, just because they like you and you work with them.

How to handle these situations? In all cases the matter must be fairly discussed so no one will be tossed out of his career undeservedly. It is usually preferable that someone closely associated with the person handle the termination, or adjustment, to avoid complicating the person's problem by a traumatic embarrassment. If there is no one, then someone who has a special place in the company should take the time and ease the news to the person, with reassurances of goodwill and appreciation, both for the work done and for the persons's suffering. Usually the director of personnel is the one delegated this type of responsibility, and is the person most capable of doing it well. It is in the worst taste to brutally cut the person off from his or her job in a case like this without plenty of psychological cushioning.

SICK AT WORK

It is not polite to go into work if you have a contagious disease, or even a disease which is so debilitating that you scare people by your condition. A virus or flu is very easily passed around, and although there is no way of knowing who gets it from whom, it's not right to go into an office situation when you are sure you are contagious.

Diseases such as hepatitis do expose the whole office to the infection and cause your co-workers the inconvenience of having to have inoculations, plus the pressure of wondering if they picked it up from you. If you are not fully recovered from such a disease, take the time to restore your strength, since it makes people very uneasy to watch someone who has been ill moving like death's specter through the office. They wonder constantly if they will have to watch out for you if you have a relapse. Don't subject people to your recovery out of some sense of duty.

THE DRINKS ARE NOT FREE

There are few problems that are more distressing to deal with in the office situation than alcoholism. When the head of the operation is an alcoholic and he or she brings the problem into the office, things can become very exasperating. Many people, of course, drink and perform their jobs well so that there isn't an imposition placed on their co-workers. It is surprising, however, when one finds a person putting in perhaps two sober hours a day at a job and holding a position of authority.

The problem of etiquette, or rather the burden of etiquette, falls on the people who work for or with alcoholics. People closely associated with them experience a growing disgust, even when they basically like and respect them. A resentment builds and it becomes difficult to maintain one's good manners when regular bouts of drunkenness are part of the workday.

One man we know, who holds a position heading up an organization, goes to lunch every day and comes back drunk every day. He makes commitments—since the lunches are usually business meetings—and forgets he has made them. He has an excellent secretary who no longer goes out of her way to cover for him.

"She doesn't actually come out on the phone and say, 'He can't talk because he's swackered,'" an associate told us, "but she doesn't go to any special pains to protect him anymore either."

The sad fact is that there is no polite way to deal with someone who is drunk. The only thing that can be done is to ignore the fact of his or her problem during the sober times, and work around the body otherwise.

Eventually these people are asked to leave, unless there is so much sentiment about them at management levels that the company deems it worthwhile to accommodate them. Sometimes a window opens, and the company will take the opportunity to retire them gracefully. For instance, the person may ask for a leave of absence, and the company will insist he resign instead.

Alcoholism brought into the office is more than rude: it lays a heavy burden on people who have a right to expect that they should be free of such pressure. Even when alcoholics are not drunk in the office, they may cause problems related to their disease. I worked for several months with a man whom I enjoyed very much and became fast friends with in the office. We used to kid him about his hang-up about bad breath because he would use so much Binaca that it was like spraying for roaches.

Eventually his work began to fall apart, he would disappear afternoons, and eventually he was fired because he was not delivering on the job at all. It turned out to be alcoholism. It was then that we realized how much discomfort the teasing about Binaca must have caused him. He was, of course, trying to cover the smell of liquor. During his short time there his assistant was doing all of his work to cover for him, since his alcohol problem made him too insecure to function even when sober.

It was a tribute to his assistant's grace and sensibilities that she never during or afterward referred to the fact that she was actually doing two jobs. People do become too polite at the wrong times: it is necessary to remember that in a business situation, if everyone isn't carrying his share of the job, the operation won't work. To try to protect someone who never will be able to perform at all is misplaced etiquette. The situation must be brought forth and discussed and a solution discovered. It can be done gracefully.

DRUGS, TOO?

Cocaine and marijuana, it has been admitted at last, are in common use among those who can afford them. The hazards of drug use of any kind are so well known that it seems odd that the people of the most awareness spend the most money on the stuff. Whatever the morality, legality, or sensibility of it, people use drugs, and the problems associated with the situation go beyond etiquette in business. Etiquette, however, is our concern here, and it is about the same as with alcoholics.

The difference is that it is not always easy to identify a problem as drug-related. Many people use marijuana as regularly as they use toothpaste and are "buzzed" all the time. They function in that state, or misfunction, depending on the effects. Cocaine users may use the white powder only on social occasions, but it is naive to think so. People who use mood elevators or depressants, legal or otherwise, or use speed to stay high through the workday cause the most problems to other people. Cocaine, for all its hazards, doesn't seem to impinge on the work of other people. The user is the affected one.

The effects of many drugs may be to make the users basically bad-tempered, short of patience, difficult to deal with, and foggy of perception. In such cases they may make it difficult for others to rely on them. This is not always the case, since many high achievers are also heavy drug users.

Because the use of so many drugs has become fashionable, one may be faced with the decision of accepting or refusing to indulge in a snort, a sniff, or a hit at business-related affairs. Some people consider it extremely rude to refuse a social drink when offered (although it's not), but no one considers it rude to refuse to take a drug.

In some industries gifts of cocaine are now considered freebies used to cultivate favors from certain people. If you do not wish to be on the receiving end of such an illegal gift, there is no rudeness in refusing. You should make it clear to the giver without becoming self-righteous that you do not want to be offered drugs again. If you want to discontinue doing business with the person, you have the right to do so on that basis.

It becomes a matter of etiquette not to "do" drugs in the office for several reasons. Some companies may come under legal investigation because business rivals may report the rumor of drug use in the office. It has happened and makes life difficult for everyone employed by the company, since the authorities involved don't discriminate among individuals. The company as a whole becomes suspect. It is not fair to expose your non-drug-using co-workers to this kind of legal shadow. It also is rude to let it be known that you do drugs in the office, because many people may find it childish behavior and an indication that you lack discretion in all matters if you must get stoned to get through a normal day's work.

If you want to use drugs, use them away from the office, or at least away from sight and knowledge. This includes taking prescription mood changers as well. If you do take prescription drugs that affect your mood, however, it should be made known discreetly to your co-workers. If you do not take drugs and you know someone who does, it is important to ignore this fact totally unless the habit affects your job. In that case, you have the right to require a change, exactly as you would in the case of an alcoholic co-worker.

It is bad practice, rather than bad manners, to keep drugs in your desk or in the office at all. This exposes you to legal prosecution or provides a reason to dismiss you.

4

WOMEN AT WORK

THE FACT THAT women are well into the process of successfully taking their place in all phases of business, from blue-collar jobs to high executive positions, has scrambled the rules of etiquette during the nine-to-five day. For women themselves the solution is simple: Treat women just as you would treat men in business. For a man, the visual impact of a woman automatically makes him want to defer, to hold doors, to pull out chairs. For women whose minds are on things other than who should walk on the street side of the sidewalk, these courtly amenities come sometimes as a jolt, sometimes as an irritation, and often as condescension.

One of the things that makes men and women somewhat uncomfortable is the fact that the old-style manners were set up around the time that Scarlett O'Hara was selling lumber. Today, in a business situation, men and women must be viewed as talents and employees, not as male and female. That alone puts us in a quandary. There is little doubt that during rush hour it is no longer expected that a man get up, tip his hat, and offer a woman his seat on the bus—unless she's on crutches or obviously pregnant. Even a mature woman might be somewhat offended if someone offered her a seat in deference to her gray hair, when she is vital enough to tackle a job every morning.

In a business setting, everyone should be treated with equal courtesy, whether man, woman, subordinate, peer, or superior. There is never a substitute for good manners; they should be a natural part of dealing with people at work or in private. If you start acting politely to someone only because she is a woman, the approach is wrong just on that basis.

It is rather demeaning to turn on your good manners for a woman. You are then saying something very different to her than "I respect you." You are saying she is somehow unable to get around without your special help.

There are three approaches men take to women in business. There are the men who open so many doors, hold so many chairs, and take so many arms that the women want to start screaming hysterically for a little space. There are the men who purposely bait women in business on so many irrelevant points that it becomes embarrassing for everyone. And there are the men who don't worry about it, who do not accept or reject women as women but see them as either talented or not, interesting or not, good or poor workers. The third is, of course, the ideal. People in business are to be viewed only in terms of what they can do and how well they can do it.

What do women want most in business? Primarily to be taken seriously. To be listened to as if their words emanate from an intelligent mind, and to be believed—which translates, to be accepted or rejected on skill. One's work record should be recognized as an indication of talent and skill. Logic and common sense should count for something.

What do they usually get? One forty-year-old executive summed it up this way: "They either hate me or they think I'm cute. Some people insinuate that I got where I am through my ability to use someone's libido, when I'm sitting in a job that was voted into being and I'm doing it almost single-handedly." No woman likes to hear a suggestion that she is making fifty thousand dollars a year because she's cute and knows how to make it pay. Any man—or woman—who suggests it, either to her or in gossip, deserves to be set straight. If a woman does get to such a position in that manner, she won't be there very long.

BEING A WOMAN

The question comes up, How do you maintain your femininity while moving ahead? And how does a man remember that an executive is still a woman while relating to her in business?

There is no problem here at all. The woman never loses femininity by being a successful business person. Thinking that such success somehow robs you of femininity is wrong to begin with. Just because a woman didn't do this at the turn of the century doesn't mean she has lost something that makes her a woman now. If she starts smoking cigars and wearing pinstripe suits and rep ties, she may look masculine, but she certainly is still a woman.

The best way to retain femininity is not to think about it. Be yourself all the way. If you want to marry and lead a life as a mother as well, fine. But don't go through the old clichés about your not being a woman unless . . . The best executive women make their choices and go with them happily and without questioning them.

A man can best treat a woman as a woman by respecting her talent, and not trying to act as if she needed help getting across the street without a male guide. In business the greatest compliment to pay anyone is to treat her as a valid, functioning person and to show your respect for her as a colleague. The rest takes care of itself. The only difference in dealing with the opposite sex in business is that you may eventually marry a colleague.

Self-respect and respect for others are both expressed the same way: with sincerity and good manners and appropriate behavior. If you remember that last word—*appropriate*—a woman will never have to worry about losing femininity, or a man worry about treating a woman badly.

PATERNALISM

Just about all the women executives I have encountered express resentment at older male executives treating them as their little girls rather than as serious adult professionals. This resentment toward "paternalism" is widespread, even when there is appreciation for the chance to move ahead.

"It's infuriating," says one young woman, "but it's also easy to slip into. And it works, too." The problem as it's seen is that these men are uncomfortable with women and fall back into a way of relating that they are familiar with. If an executive has related to women only as wives, mothers, or daughters, he will automatically treat a younger woman as a daughter if he wants to help her career. This is very difficult for the woman, who naturally enough sees herself as an adult trying to get ahead on her creative merit.

Not to be taken seriously by one's boss is extremely frustrating. The older male executive can point out that he also behaves in an avuncular manner toward younger men, but in fact this feeling takes a more professional turn, and very few men will treat other men in the playful, teasing way that raises the hackles of young executive women.

Men get better breaks, are taken more seriously, and are more likely to receive the "golden boy" treatment from older men. Some women get similar treatment, but it appears that the dues they pay are more humiliating than the ones required from younger men.

Some women manage to buck this by taking on more masculine characteristics, reading up on the sports pages, and taking approaches that allow older men to feel less of a sex difference and to be more themselves. Some of these women go so far as to adopt mannish suits and to take pains never to appear as traditionally "feminine." They are not lesbians, necessarily, but feel that sacrificing parts of their apparent femininity in the career area helps them move ahead more quickly. It seems to work, although this is most likely due to their high ambition and drive for success.

One way to wean an older male boss from paternalism and into a more serious way of relating is to make him comfortable with you. If his basic approach comes out of a confusion about what to do with you, since he has mostly dealt with women as secretaries or receptionists, it is up to you to set the standard for something new.

Give the man a way to relate to you. Be extremely businesslike while not sacrificing what you are. Point him constantly toward your talent, don't wait for him to notice. Refer to your successes. Ask his advice seriously. It is impossible for anyone not to become comfortable immediately when asked to talk about what he knows best. Asking advice is the best comforter there is, and you can only win by doing it. When someone gives you advice he will tell you more about himself in a few minutes than you can get from a year of observation. Once you have broken the barrier and he is open to you, other avenues can open up as bases of relating as executive colleagues rather than surrogate father/daughter.

It is best not to relate out of resentment or in spite of something. In this situation the way that breaks open a true business relationship is the best way.

Not all woman feel that paternalism is a pattern—some see it more as an individual personality quirk. Others say that the business world is nothing but paternalism, and it has nothing to do with being female.

"The biggest trap for women to fall into," says one highly successful woman exec, "is to assume that whatever happens to you is because you're a woman. Put yourself in the other person's place instead of reacting emotionally to your first impressions. Don't make your boss a victim of your own projections. Gauge the person you are working with and gear yourself to work with him at your best.

"Any well-run company advances people on merit—that is still the only thing that matters. When you are moving up it doesn't matter what sex, age, race you are. As for paternalism, any young person is in a sense following in the footsteps of an older executive in a child/parent way. That relationship is the basis of all adult relationships. You can't waste time fuming about it."

In business, women are the same as men. It is not only courtesy but professionalism to show empathy for a person's position and problems. Don't come on like a resentful child when someone becomes paternalistic. Explain in detail why you feel a problem exists and say how you feel it can be solved. Professional behavior will always lead people away from emotional cushions. If you act like an adult, your boss will by necessity have to start treating you like one.

VOICES OF AUTHORITY

How does a woman react to unfair treatment? "Usually with fury and a sharp tongue," says one executive woman. This can work very well if the woman is in a certain area where it's hard to get good people. A valid sharp criticism from a highly talented woman can be as effective as a soft remark from William Paley. It is difficult to ascertain the etiquette here. Some high-pressure jobs, such as those in medical centers, demand fast action. In most business settings, however, any woman who can cultivate a reputation for being cool and controlled under pressure will have a happier career overall.

"Our voices are high and shrill when we become angry," one woman pointed out. "People don't listen to that kind of thin sound as the voice of authority. That's why I think women are better off using what might be called women's ways to get their point across. It's more appropriate; it's never wrong to use good manners; and you don't have the men around calling you a bitch behind your back."

"Women's ways" in this case certainly does not mean playing up to a male in a seductive or childish way. Women are most effective when being straightforwardly feminine, not shouting, but speaking firmly and directly. Men also are more effective in this way, but when a man with a strong voice raises it, the effect is more intimidating than a high-pitched sound.

It is never good to shout in business. One cultivates more respect by dealing rationally. Anyone who must scream her way through a business day should reevaluate her effectiveness and her approach, and decide what she is doing wrong.

AGGRESSIVENESS

Aggressiveness is one of the tools that are required for advancing in the corporate structure. Yet when women are aggressive they are automatically labeled "bitch" or "unfeminine." It's ridiculous to expect a woman to sit at her desk like a southern belle waiting for a gentleman caller when a supplier is messing up a deadline. It is also foolish to expect anyone not to use drive and determination—and aggressiveness—to try to move ahead at a proper pace when she's pursuing a career. There is nothing incorrect about a woman using "male tactics" to advance her career and to do a better job.

LEFT OUT

One action that women dislike and which is outright rude is to be excluded from a discussion when they are standing right there, very much a part of the group. It is common courtesy not to exclude a person from a conversation if she is standing with you.

It is true that men are naturally comfortable talking with one another because of what one woman called male bonding. The adjustment to including women as peers in their conversation makes them somewhat uncomfortable. But once the adjustment is made, no one really notices the difference. Part of this discomfort comes from the old idea that you can't use certain language in front of women which you can use with men—the old "not for mixed company" ploy.

The truth is that women are no more offended by commonly used profanities or slang then men. It is basically crude to rely on cusswords, but any woman who has been to the movies in the past ten years has heard them all at least twice. Most women think it is absurd and annoying that men even consider female ears delicate anymore. One woman, who is a vice-president of a large company, said that the men who get carried away and say "damn" or "shit" at a meeting will suddenly pull back and apologize to her. "I al-

ways want to say, 'What the hell, I use the fucking word myself.' "
But she doesn't.

It is an annoyance to be singled out as Shirley Temple at a business meeting, and to do it to someone is more rude than using a simple accepted "bad word."

When people say that certain behavior doesn't look good on a woman, they are really saying that it doesn't look good on anyone. Why should anyone think, for instance, that swearing at people and using vulgar language should be more acceptable coming from a man than from a woman? A foul mouth is unacceptable in any business situation.

It is one thing to say, "I wish I had brought the damn report along with me," in a meeting with your day-to-day colleagues. It is something else to call your secretary and say, "Bring that goddamn report up here right now."

Some women mistakenly think if they use foul language regularly it makes them somehow more effective in business. But no one can be effective at any executive level by commonly using offensive, crude language.

PARTY TIME

The dividing line between the sexes is most often apparent at social functions or at conventions. I knew one woman who was so successfully a part of an otherwise all-male department that there was no place she was left out. Her boss would take his girlfriend, not his wife, to out-of-town meetings, and even this situation did not cause an exclusion. She just brought her boyfriend along.

At parties for the office and in business in general, the complaint is that men politick with each other, using the opportunity to do business of some kind, but become flirtatious with women whether they're at the same corporate level or not.

In such a case the woman can initiate the political approach herself, effectively defusing the coyness and bumping the conversation into the business area she wants to discuss. This abrupt psychological move will have a positive result, especially if the woman is astute about her subject, and the mood will follow the road she's taking. There is nothing rude about this; fast subject changes and brief conversational exchanges are the rule at parties.

This approach also works well when men exclude a woman from a conversation when she is standing with them. Unless it truly is none of her business, she has a right to assume that the talk is meant to include her. By taking her cue naturally, without making a point of forcing her way into the talk with the attitude that she has been left out and is determined to be included, she can take part in any discussion that should include her.

It is rude to force your way into a chat that does not include you, however. In many situations—especially at parties—two people in a group of three may get on a subject that excludes the third. That is a cue for the third person to be mute, or to smile and move away.

INTRODUCTIONS

Worse than being left out of a peer-level conversation is being ignored during a round of introductions. One woman mentioned her boss, who treats all the women at the office like fragile, helpless decorations. But he never introduces any of them to a visitor in the office when he is introducing the men. "It's as if we aren't there or don't have enough importance to be mentioned. Can you imagine how my blood boils when I'm standing there with four people and only three get introduced?"

The women have complained about it to their boss countless times, but his concept of women as office furniture is so ingrained that he doesn't change.

OTHER WOMEN

There is a complaint from some quarters that women who have made it to the top don't reach down to help younger women the way older men help junior male execs. The attitude, it is said, seems to be that since they had to claw their way to the top, they feel that the newer women can do it that way as well. Other women claim that they do receive help and decent treatment from women at upper levels. Again, both may be true depending on the woman.

A lot of executive women think some secretaries try to live "the myth of the little woman" at the office. But in general women executives and women secretaries get along tremendously well and have excellent business relationships. They can also communicate on peer levels at certain points, which is something male bosses generally can't do unless they're the same age, more or less, as their secretaries.

COMPLIMENTS

It is difficult for a man not to comment when a woman looks especially good. It seems to be acceptable for a woman in an office to tell another woman she looks wonderful, but if a man does it his motive may be mistaken. If a man is at a social gathering with a female colleague, he can express appreciation of her appearance more effusively than at the office. In the office, it is best to limit compliments to a woman's work and save the courtly behavior for other times.

Some suggest if a woman dresses in soft, ultrafeminine clothes she will appreciate personal compliments; if she is a conservative dresser, choosing outfits that play down beauty or noticeability, stick to business. As we say elsewhere in this book, it is somewhat ridiculous to compliment anyone on wearing clothes that are dictated by the rules of conservative business. It would be like complimenting a female paratrooper on her uniform.

"I'LL DO IT"

Many women resent being "done for" these days, seeing it as condescension. It should be remembered that good manners are never degrading to either party, and it is rude to refuse an honest courtesy in a business situation. You can define your career by performance and advancement, but not by publicly reproving a man who is trying to be polite.

It is as rude for a man not to offer similar courtesies to other men, such as holding doors, when the occasion indicates it. In this case common business courtesy dictates treating men and women with equal politeness. And a man should never get into a hassle about which one should hold the door. If someone holds the door for you nod politely and go in. An entrance is no place to show who is the most masculine man. Any man who has true self-respect can accept as well as perform common courtesies.

One courtesy that men do for women is cigarette lighting. This is something that should only be done socially, unless the man is also lighting up at the same time as the woman and the woman is next to him. It is inconvenient to continually flash a flame under a woman's nose every time she puts a cigarette to her mouth. Normally she performs this act without thinking about it, and suddenly she is being threatened with a lit torch out of nowhere. In business, women light their own, unless two or more people are having a smoke. In this case it should not be assumed that the man does the lighting; either sex may do the honors.

If a man is going to offer a light, he should ask first if he may. The woman who wants to handle her own light can say, "Thanks, but I have it," when she sees a man reach for the matches. Nothing is more ludicrous than seeing a man reach for the lighter every time a woman reaches for a cigarette.

CHAIR PULLERS

Women don't usually object to traditional acts of courtesy in themselves, such as holding the chair or the door, but they do become annoyed when they feel that men do these things only because they are women. Anyone will hold a door for anyone else as a natural form of courtesy, but some men act as if a woman has to be taken care of, like some fragile thing that might break.

Some men even have some deep-seated feeling that women are

not strong enough to do certain things. They equate muscle strength with males and not with females.

Some men deliberately avoid opening doors for women in business situations, which also highlights the fact that they are making a point about it. The rule is to be natural: if you think it's appropriate to do a courtesy for a woman, do it; if not, don't.

One woman executive told me she hates walking into a company meeting because all the men there stand up when she enters the room. She finds it embarrassing since they don't do it for other men. It is not polite to stand for women and not for men. In a business situation it is not necessary to stand for anyone, except the President of the United States if he should walk in.

Another woman executive from another company said, "Tell her she's lucky. I'm always worried they'll pull the chair out from under me at our company."

Some etiquette about deferring to women holds in business. If a woman is having a struggle to remove her coat or sweater while sitting, it is common courtesy for a man or woman sitting next to her to aid the action. It is not necessary to get up and go around the room to her chair just to help her, unless she is in a wheelchair. And then you would ask first if she needs help.

It is a nice gesture to hold her chair for her, but only if you are both about to be seated at the same time. It is not necessary to rise from a conference table, nor to hold the chair for a woman in a business situation. If any woman demands or implies that she expects such courtesies, she is in the wrong, and her wishes can be ignored.

It would be rude for a man to allow a woman to be embarrassed by not picking up something she dropped or refusing to help her out of a situation that she plainly cannot handle on her own. If her skirt becomes caught in a chair, if the chair is somehow stuck and she cannot get it loose and is carrying things—these situations demand assistance, and any man who sits and enjoys a woman's discomfiture, as it it were a revenge for her being in business, is acting less than a man.

Most women feel that appropriateness of behavior is the only consideration that should be made. If a woman is laden with packages or going to lunch with you, or if you just like holding doors for people, then do it. But not because she is a woman.

Reader's Digest once reported the famous story about the woman who said to a man:

"Please don't hold the door because I'm a lady."

He answered, "I'm not—I do it because I'm a gentleman."

That sums it up best.

UP, DOWN, AND AROUND

The new etiquette in relation to women can almost be summed up in elevators and revolving doors. I was at lunch one day and heard two young male execs talking about what to do when you get to a revolving door with a woman. Who goes first? Who does the pushing of the door? And how do you do it without wrecking your fingers or stumbling over the lady?

There is no set rule for revolving doors, but here are the suggestions I've collected:

If the woman is first, she goes in first and pushes, and the man follows and pushes his door.

The man says or indicates that he will push for her and lets her go in first, while he takes the door behind and pushes it.

There is no reason why a woman should go first, but in our society we always assume that she will, so things become less awkward if we go with that convention. The point is not that the woman or the man goes first, but that they go through the doors easily. Don't give confusing signals. If the woman starts reaching for her own door, a man shouldn't interfere. A woman is certainly strong enough to push a door open.

If two women are at a door, the one in the higher position or the one who is considerably older goes first, and the younger or lesser one follows.

If you are at a very busy revolving door, the thing is probably whirling at a fast clip. Let the woman get in, and follow immediately if you can. It is likely in today's rude society, however, that another woman—or man—may push in front of you and your companion will have to wait inside for you. No embarrassment or comment is needed. Just smile and treat it as a humorous mix-up.

Elevators present another area of confusion. If a man is standing first at an elevator in front of several other people, male and female, he enters first rather than stand blocking the way to allow women in. If you want to be in the front of the elevator, get in and take a position by the operating bank, out of the way, or place yourself back farther in the crowd. When getting off an elevator, one never stands aside inside the car just to allow women to exit first. You stand aside only if you are not getting off at that floor. The consideration of the needs of the whole group comes before good manners to any single person on the elevator.

In elevators and doorways, women often place their so-called prerogative to go first above good manners. Women should not automatically assume that they have first rights to enter any doorway or passageway. I have often seen a woman start walking, or keep moving nonstop, brushing past an unsuspecting man who didn't even see her, just to "go in first." This is annoying, irritating, and rude.

If a woman does make such an assumption and pushes aside a man, she should say, "Excuse me"; it is usually not polite for the man to publicly take her to task for her bad manners, although many men will voice a sarcastic "excuse me" to the woman if they are annoyed enough. This is not polite either. It is as bad to point out bad manners to someone as it is to practice them in the first place.

During the days before paved streets, when animals and flying mud were a hazard to pedestrians, it was considered impolite to let a woman walk on the curb side of the sidewalk. This convention, based on a protective attitude toward women in hobble skirts, is no longer needed and need not be observed at all. It is in fact not feasible to walk along a busy city street changing sides every couple of blocks and interrupting your conversation just to maintain the outer lane. Few men do this anymore, and it certainly has no place in a business situation.

It is still good manners for a man to hold the door of a cab or a car for a woman if he is getting in with her. It is nice, but not necessary, to go around to her side to let her in if you are driving. It looks great to do so, and is a nice way of expressing your respect for her as a human being. The way to do it is to keep the car locked so you can unlock her door first, then go around and let yourself in.

In a dangerous area, or in a parking lot at night, it is required that a man make sure a woman is inside the car safely before getting into the car. He should never leave a woman standing alone outside the car in such a situation unless he knows she is better able to defend herself than he is. If that sounds a touch chauvinistic, remember that criminals are much more likely to attack a woman than to go after a man, even if she is with him.

It is not necessary, or even considered acceptable by some women, for a man who is driving to come around and open the door to help a woman passenger out of the car. Some women find it embarrassing, and it does seem ludicrous in today's society to go through such a performance. If the woman is wearing a very fussy formal dress, or there is some reason why it is difficult for her to get out of a car on her own, then of course the man should come around and help. In normal situations the woman can do it herself.

The reason why it is a nice touch to open the car door for her so she can get in, and not to help her exit, is simple: it follows naturally and easily. The man can unlock the door on her side, let her in, and go around. She can unlock his door from inside if it is easy to do and won't set off a burglar alarm.

If you are a man walking with a woman and you are carrying some bulky item, it is up to her to take the lead and hail the cab, open the doors for you, and see that you are safe from pushers and shovers as best she can. She pushes the elevator buttons, holds the elevator doors open, and gets you to your common destination.

RELAX

The core of the problem between men and women relating on a business level is the inability of some men to relax with women. They can't get past the idea that they are somehow on a first date even though they are in an office, and they try to approach women to impress them. There is no reason for a man to have to impress a woman or to make her like him from a sexual point of view in an office. Too many men try to preserve an opening to keep alive the possibility of relating as men and women rather than as working colleagues. If the man-woman thing is meant to happen, it will anyway. But it helps everyone relax if it can be put aside from nine to five.

5

WHEN CUPID
GETS STUPID

SEX IS SO much fun away from the office that it seems unfair to proscribe it at work. Work is a perfect place to meet people and get to know them before taking a chance on dating. Many people even look for jobs with particular companies because of the opportunities to meet members of the opposite sex (or the same sex, if that's the kind of place it is). For many young people the working place is their only suitable avenue for meeting romantic partners and future mates.

There is nothing objectionable about people meeting, falling in love, and taking it from there in an office situation. Love is where you find it, after all. The problem arises when the people spend much of the workday pursuing love.

One should not necessarily avoid romantic possibilities just because they occur in the office, but one should be discreet in approaching them. Serious, aboveboard dating is acceptable in just about any situation. Looking for casual sexual dalliance, using the office as a source of frivolous, superficial affairs or carrying on with as many of your co-workers as you can like some sort of office alley cat is never proper business conduct.

It should always be remembered that casual sexual activity almost always leads to trouble in the office. It leads to gossip; it may even lead to deterioration of office morale if key people are involved. And it too often leads to someone getting fired. Serious sexual/romantic liaisons based on a real emotional feeling may have a better chance of being passed over by Old Man Trouble, but not always. Even a true romance, handled improperly, can lead to the end of the road for promising careers.

The big problem with sexual affairs in the office is not so much that they are a breach of etiquette—the etiquette lies more in how they are handled—as that they disrupt work, jeopardize careers of people not involved, and can damage company credibility if any of the affairs becomes a cause for scandal. This becomes particularly true when the romance involves the head of the company and a promising newcomer. The youngster is moved ahead, promoted over people who have more ability or more experience, and receives favors from the company that would not normally be available to someone at that point in his or her career. If the company happens to be large and powerful, such liaisons may even be reported as news. This happened when Mary Cunningham was promoted too quickly at Bendix Corporation and was forced to resign in the face of scandal. It was emphatically denied that there was any romantic base for her fast career rise, but later on she married the boss.

Lower-level affairs also can have demoralizing effects on co-workers—even if no careers are put in jeopardy. Any secret love affair involves two people who are in an unusual emotional state, and they will necessarily perform in ways that are often unexplainable. People in love—or deeply infatuated—do not always act in a rational manner. Decisions are made based on the feeling of love that exists; petty resentments may keep one or both of them seesawing between ecstasy and depression. And jealousy may become a motivating factor in relating to other people in the office.

When the affair involves a higher-level person in authority and someone who reports to a boss below that first person, things can become very unpleasant indeed. The innocent boss in the middle becomes trampled between the person above him and the person below. He loses his authority and finds himself being blamed and reprimanded and his authority flouted. Eventually it occurs that the young lover below the two bosses is making the real decisions, and things begin to fall apart. And through it all the real problem is never mentioned: there would be no hassle if there were no love affair going on. It becomes like a huge hole in the floor that is covered by a pretty oriental carpet. Everyone pretends they don't want to ruin the carpet by walking on it, but the truth is they don't want to fall through the hole.

HOW TO HANDLE THE LOVER

How do you handle a situation where you are being affected adversely by someone else's love affair? Etiquette says you must smile, nod, and not talk about the fact of the affair. But that rule of good taste holds only as long as you are not losing career ground in any way. If you are unable to exercise your authority to get a job done, if you see yourself as in charge and your boss's lover sees you as unemployed, then you must set aside this rule of silence and take steps to save your career.

The first step is to confer with your boss—the high-level partner in the affair—and set forth your complaints without mentioning that you know about the affair. If you feel that your authority has deteriorated to a drastic enough point, you may even suggest that the younger lover be fired or transferred to another department. The boss will probably try to get you to iron out the differences, then privately tell the lover to be more cooperative.

If this works out, then the problem is solved and no one is embarrassed. The situation will not be ideal, because it is almost impossible for the lover to revert once he or she has been given so much freedom. Only an unusually mature person can handle it; and if the person were that mature in the first place, no problem would have arisen.

If the young lover continues to make problems and does not

shape up, then you must make the difficult choice of either waiting hopefully until the affair ends, or forcing the issue and demanding that a clear resolution be made to resolve the matter—in your favor. You can use your knowledge of the affair as a lever, but you must also be aware that you may make an enemy of your own boss by doing so. The thing in your favor is that people in these situations do not always act in their own best interests; two people involved in such an affair are at a disadvantage just because one lover is favoring the other.

When you are bringing the issue to a confrontation, always try to refrain from saying anything that will make the boss lose face. Use the tools of etiquette as weapons of diplomacy, not of battle. Yes, you can be ready to lash out about the unfairness of the situation and the lack of judgment on the boss's part in having allowed the situation to get out of hand. But it is more to your advantage to suggest solutions that are amicable and benefit all parties concerned, rather than to demand retribution. Even if the young lover must be fired or forced to resign, approach it as a business move that is regrettable, rather than as justice done. When the affair has ended, the boss will remember that you stood by him and helped him (or her) find a graceful, quiet solution, despite the fact that you went through some bad times. This can only work to your own advantage overall.

Never stoop to personal attacks; do not try to discredit the younger lover. This won't work in the first place, and if the younger one is really unlikable, the older lover will eventually realize it. No matter what you may feel personally, keep your complaints on a business level. Do not place a wedge between them on the emotional issue. You can fight for your job, but there is no reason to care if they continue their affair. Your only course of action should be to remove an obstacle from your career, not to do a hatchet job on two people acting foolishly.

Things that are fair to mention regarding the romance include imparting the information that other people in the office know and are gossiping about it; that the younger lover may be offensive to everyone because he or she thinks the romance provides an immunity against being fired; that the situation is disrupting too much productivity in the office to warrant an attitude of benevolent neglect.

I know of one advertising executive who had a penchant for having minor affairs with young women execs. Privately he would promise them creative freedom and treat them as golden girls while the romance ran hot. It caused problems for the lower-level managers who were unable to effectively control the young geniuses. The pattern was that the young lover would begin playing prima donna, displaying temperament and demanding full freedom in all things. This would go on for a few difficult months; then someone would complain or find out what the problem was, and there would be a wasted month of trying to persuade the boss to fire the lover. When the older exec finally lost romantic interest, the lower boss had the final satisfaction of firing the obnoxious lover.

Because the big boss was usually able to keep the affair secret for a while, and he usually was attracted to talented women, he was able to carry on as much as he wanted. But things almost always come to a point of battle when top-level executives are unable to control their emotions or physical appetites enough to be prudent in their love affairs.

Whatever you attempt when trying to save your own career, it is probably always best not to try to attack the big boss. Most companies will stand behind high-level execs in cases like this and you will only damage your own future and make a powerful enemy. If, on the other hand, someone higher up approaches you and asks you to take over your boss's job, it is perfectly all right to accept.

REMAINING PURE

A final thing to remember about any in-office affair is this: If it does not stand in the way of your own career and does not interfere with the performance of your job duties, keep out of it. Do not gossip about it; do not try to make political hay out of it; don't let the parties to it know you are aware of the affair, unless one of them chooses to confide in you. And if one does confide in you, do not let yourself be placed in a position of having to defend, protect, or conceal the secret.

PREDATORS

In any office where there are men and women you'll find predators looking for sexual gratification wherever it can be found—and there are few offices where it can't be found. One of the most uncomfortable situations of this type that I heard of involved a sales manager who developed a predatory attraction for a young married woman who was a secretary in another department. Because she was an effusive, bright, and very outgoing person, her personality enhanced an already attractive physical appearance. There was almost no one who wasn't somewhat entranced by her. The sales manager just happened to be particularly entranced.

Jean always greeted everyone with a smile and a friendly, open Midwest cordiality. She soon realized that he took her general goodwill as an encouragement for him to invite her out after work. Every day he would stop in and make suggestions for a rendezvous after work, embarrassing her in front of others in the office and making her feel hassled, since she had made it clear that she was happily married.

This particular problem was resolved when the sales manager was on his way to lunch one day and pitched forward on his face, dead on the spot. But you can't always rely on something like this happening. There were two factors at work here that hindered a solution: one was the man's high position in the company; one was the secretary's inability to be rude to anyone, no matter how badly he acted.

In the case of this predator, she should have made a complaint to her boss, who was not aware of the harassment, and insisted that something be done to make it clear to the sales manager that he was way out of line. If the predator had been someone lower down the corporate ladder, she should have confronted him with her objections as soon as he became offensive. It is one thing to ask a woman in the office to go to dinner—that is more or less acceptable social behavior. It becomes offensive when the woman says she is married. For him to continue to hound her was an insult—he was assuming she could be made if the offer became attractive enough—and it gave her an extra burden to work under, since she was upset by his attentions.

In all cases, office predators should be confronted by someone—either the woman herself or her immediate superior. If nothing is done to change the situation, then she should take up the matter with personnel. The initial objections should be made in private. If the predator will not take them seriously, then there is no longer any reason to respect his reputation. Any effective steps that will stop him should be taken.

WEDDING RINGS

Some people, men especially, wear wedding bands to work as a defense against suitors or women looking for mates. In some offices, of course, it is not likely that one's true marital status will remain undiscovered. But for people who do not wish to mix business and romance, the simple tactic of wearing a wedding band is a mute signal to keep away.

People who really are married and receive sexual offers from people who are aware of this fact are not bound to be particularly polite in refusing. The marriage state is still considered to place one outside of the hunting arena, and it is extremely rude to make a pass at either a married man or woman. The simple statement, "I'm married," is all that need be said to an unwanted sexual invitation. No other rationalization is required, and it is not necessary to worry about whether or not the person is hurt by the rejection. In this case the person asks for whatever he or she gets.

When a married person makes a sexual overture, and this is much more common, refusal is not a matter of etiquette but of good sense. The facts are in and are now ancient history about married men who play around and married women who make themselves available. They usually are out for ego gratification with no strings attached. If you are willing to take a chance on the unsolvable problems attendant on having an affair with a married person, then prepare several envelopes addressed to Dear Abby. You're going to need them.

As a bottom line, however, it is as insulting for a married person to make overtures to someone in the office as it would be for him or her to receive them. An invitation to enter into any situation that will leave one vulnerable to gossip, emotional pain, or compromise is an act of rudeness.

A KISS IS STILL A KISS

A kiss on the hand may be Continental, but in business—American business—a simple handshake will do. There are times when kissing is acceptable in business, and these times are discussed later in this chapter. As a general rule, however, the only time a kiss is really acceptable between co-workers is when they are close friends greeting each other after an absence of some time.

It is surprising that kissing will come up at strange times in business situations. I was told a story by a friend who was a middle-level executive in an insurance company. He was being introduced to a new salesperson, who happened to be the first woman in her department, and who also happened to be young and attractive. Present were the men she was going to work with and her boss. My friend was introduced to her as the new addition to the staff. After he had shaken hands with two of the men present, he extended his hand to welcome her, but, instead, she moved in, saying, "You must get tired of shaking hands with all these men," and kissed him on the cheek.

It was such an unexpected act that no one really knew whether or not to be embarrassed, but it was totally out of order. Because she was new, and because no one made any big thing about it in front of her, it passed without comment. My friend said, "Thank you" with a bland smile and departed.

In some cases such an act would be destructive of the woman's image right from the first day on the job. Another person who heard the story described the woman as "waving her tits at him and she should have been reprimanded." If she had been on the job awhile, a reprimand from her boss would have been in order. It is extremely unprofessional to perform such a provocative act in a business situation.

Kissing, hugging, or any other demonstration of affection should only be performed in *appropriate* situations. Several factors determine whether or not something is appropriate—the most important being the general ambience and style of the business. A kiss that may be appropriate in an ad company may be very out of order in a law firm, for example. Some companies would even consider a hearty greeting to be somewhat out of line, whereas others take on the atmosphere of a year-round company picnic.

Kissing in business situations is appropriate in cases such as these:

- when two female colleagues meet briefly in a hectic social situation, such as a cocktail party, where interaction is necessarily rushed and must be kept superficial
- when two people meet in the office, or in any quasi-business situation, such as at lunch in a public place, and are genuinely happy to see each other
- when congratulations are in order, such as the announcement of a wedding or a baby, a promotion, or winning the state lottery
- when the situation involves two people who are close friends as well as business associates and demonstrations of friendship are commonly used between them
- when you visit someone at her office and she offers a kiss as a gesture to establish the fact that she likes you well enough to have a personal as well as a business friendship

It is still not proper for a man to make the first move toward kissing a female colleague unless there is an already established pattern. The prerogative to kiss and hug still remains with the woman in business situations.

It is no longer considered that a kiss is only something that should be used in a romantic situation, although in America this act still has enough special connotations that it should be used judiciously. It is still considered a curiosity if two men kiss in business or in public, despite the influx of foreign businessmen.

INAPPROPRIATENESS

We spoke of when it is appropriate to express affection in demonstrative terms in business. It is also useful to know when such behavior is not appropriate.

During times of crisis or problem solving, it is not correct to engage in affectionate skirmishes of welcome before, during, or right after a meeting. Keep greetings on a decorous level until you are in a situation where you can loosen up.

Avoid "public" noisy displays of kissing and hugging in the office. It is best to reserve this type of greeting for the privacy of your own office, even when your husband or wife visits.

It is seldom proper for a boss or anyone to place his or her arm around an associate. This gesture, despite the fact that it may arise from purely platonic motives, is not a proper mannerism. It is found that most people resent being "cuddled" when discussing business; and the extreme physical closeness makes it difficult to focus on the matter at hand.

It would seem that Christmas parties in the office are a time when a person has an excuse to kiss and hug a co-worker. It is not proper here to use these "open" situations as an excuse to make a sexual inroad. If the kiss and/or hug is part of an expression of gratitude toward a co-worker with whom you already have a special, warm relationship, then the gesture is not viewed as taking a liberty. But office parties should not be used to excuse satyric behavior. If you are sexually interested in a co-worker, make your desires known in more discreet, private circumstances.

HOW TO AVOID A KISS

She met me on the street on Madison Avenue, the temporary typist who had filled in for two weeks when our secretary was ill. I smiled and stopped; she smiled and sailed right up and aimed her puckered mouth at me. I brought my hand up between us, offering to shake hers, and said, "Nice to see you, Miss Johnson."

It is difficult to refuse to kiss someone who offers. It is always taken as a rejection, even when there is no reason to smooch. In our society many people do not want to expose themselves to any more possibilities of infection than necessary. Others prefer to save intimacies for intimate times. Others don't like a lot of casual close contact, touching, stroking, or holding. It is rude to challenge someone who refuses or sidesteps any sort of intimacy, especially in a business situation. Save your psychological analyses for the group session at your psychiatrist's.

If someone does offer a kiss and you don't want it, turn your mouth away and offer a cheek. Or smile and take one hand and squeeze an arm affectionately instead of puckering up at all. Or say that you have a cold sore inside your mouth and it hurts. That effectively douses the kissers, who don't want to receive infections but don't seem to mind passing them on.

If one is going to kiss another person in a business situation, it is polite to be sure not to leave a mark of makeup or a little wet spot. One cannot politely reach up and wipe away the wet after a kiss, so it is up to the kisser to make sure that the kiss is "clean," so to speak.

ONE TIME ONLY

It is almost never a good idea to go to bed with a co-worker on a one-night-stand basis. Of the two situations, having an affair or having sex once, the affair is preferable, since it leaves you knowing exactly where you stand with the person. A one-night stand leaves you with the question "Is that all there is?" standing over you. If that indeed is all, then there is a certain amount of rejection assumed by one or both of the parties. Sometimes you meet that rare person who thinks going to bed with you once was such a wonderful experience that he or she becomes a lifelong friend and will do anything for you forever. Usually there is something embarrassing about the morning after, and if you don't ask again or mention the possibility of a repeat, the person feels rebuffed.

It is better not to go to bed at all with a co-worker if you know you will want to do it only one time. If you have done it once, then try to make the offer of having dinner or lunch and letting the person know you respect her/ him, and really did enjoy her/ him as a person, and are grateful for the opportunity to have shared something nice. There is nothing bad about honest flattery and saying nice things to someone you had sex with.

If something went wrong with the attempt at sex, then it is best to expend some effort in strengthening another kind of relationship in the office to reassure both of you that it didn't matter and to get over the embarrassment that may remain. Don't refer to the actual incident. A card that says "Thanks anyway" is a good friendship builder; or a rose on the desk, or buying the coffee and roll at the break. All help reestablish normalcy and ease.

L'AFFAIRE

It happens that you may end up having an affair with a co-worker no matter how sensible you were going to be about it. You can't always buck your karma, after all. If you do, then keep it between yourselves. Don't discuss it or admit it to anyone in the office. Chances are they will find out some way, but don't let it be through either of you.

When making assignations, do it by phone, not through furtive whisperings or notes on the desk. Even if the person is in the next office, do it by phone. It will help you be more natural, and no one will have the embarrassment of discovering you. It's more fun this way, too.

Don't stop seeing the person for lunch or stop doing anything you have ever done before, even if people are gossiping. Continue as you were in public. If you are wont to give little remembrances to people in the office, they can be given to the lover. If you were wont to disagree about things workwise, continue to do so. Don't try to "play" it any way. The natural approach is best. If you accept the fact of your affair in your mind, then you can carry it off without bothering anyone else.

If people ask you if you are messing around with so and so, tell them no point-blank. You can ask them why they asked if you want clues on how to keep the affair secret.

Try not to meet during the workday, if possible, unless you would normally have lunch with your co-workers.

If you are married, it is best to keep your spouse apprised of where you purportedly will be so he or she doesn't get into calling the office to check on your whereabouts. An angry spouse calling to find you is a giveaway to someone who might have suspicions. And a person in the office who has suspicions will always ask other people if they have suspicions, and next thing you know . . .

While some affairs mature into serious relationships, most of them only produce ex-lovers. Some people can't handle the fact that a lover has gone on to someone else. In a casual affair, remember, one of you is lying and one of you is in love to a certain extent. This is not so in a real love affair, but a sexual relationship usually has two people in love with the same person. No matter how mild that feeling may be, it is there. Even if it is based totally on ego gratification, it is there. People become very possessive about their sexual conquests and do not like to see someone else getting what they no longer have—even when they're done with it.

I knew of one man who had a wife and children at home and also liked to have trifling affairs at work. The problem came about when one ex-affair started calling his wife to tell her all about the current affair, and the wife started coming to the office with her sister in tow, purposely to cut the other woman dead. It was not pretty.

YOU'RE ON YOUR OWN

No one should ever expect a co-worker or a secretary to cover for him if he is having a love affair, either in the office or out. Only by keeping it secret from your co-workers can they be free of the probings by your family.

The way to handle things is to say, "If my wife calls, please tell her I'll call her at such and such a time." If you are the one who gets the call and the caller questions you further, just say you don't know anything else and have to get off the line for business reasons. Claim to have someone in the office or to be on your way to a meeting, but don't offer solace, information, or speculation.

AFTER THE BALL IS OVER

Office affairs, just like those in real life, often follow the pattern of a courtship, and one or both persons may really fall in love. Then one or both persons may fall out of love and the affair ends. It happened in one case that a young man started dating a woman of his own age after meeting her at a company party. She worked in another department. They dated seriously for about a year, and she even accompanied him to his family gatherings. Then he stopped asking her out. Later he married someone else. The first woman, however, had fallen in love with him and was silently waiting for him to come back to her, popular fiction–style. Fortunately, a friend she confided in was able to suggest some therapy and she got over it and went on to a better career and social life.

The point to remember here is that dating a person from the office does not mean that the same emotional processes will not occur that would if you met through some other agency. When dating anyone through the office, it is best to examine your feelings from the start and be honest about them. If you want to date casually over an indefinite period and expect no reciprocal emotional feelings to exist, make it clear every step of the way. Many young people who are not yet performing at the executive level may use their companies as hunting grounds for dates. It is not an unhealthy attitude. It's not like singles bars where people are looking for sex only. The basis for forming a good relationship is better because you are more likely to meet someone with similar background and interests at work than anywhere else.

Many young people also feel it is good because pressure doesn't exist here as it does in social meeting places. You can get to know someone for several weeks or months before you decide to date, and by that time you have enough in common that the date won't be strained. If you want to continue to see each other, you can; if not, the work can be used as a cover for future commitments.

THE SEXUAL CONQUISTADOR

The male on the make is still very much a part of the business situation, even though many men are becoming reticent about sexual aggressiveness as the new woman emerges more definitely as a professional competitor instead of a consort. There will always be a man in every office who must hone his sexual mettle in a way that is tiresome to most of the women he lights on. Sexual innuendo, veiled or blatant, coming from either a man or a woman, is extremely annoying. People who make insinuating or overt sexual remarks, who may even use their hands to reinforce these statements, become a real problem in the office.

If the sexual conquistador has had enough success to stimulate his appetites, then there will be no stopping him. Mostly this type of rudeness takes the form of spoken sexual implication, usually by twisting every innocent remark or occasion into one with sexual overtones that were never intended.

For example, a woman might be complaining that the size of her studio apartment makes it difficult to entertain people at home. The conquistador would immediately say something like "I think it would be fun to be entertained by you in such an intimate place."

The woman, blushing, might parry with "Well, believe me, it gets boring having to stack people on top of each other when they come to dinner."

And he returns with "I wouldn't get bored being stacked with you."

It goes on *ad nauseam,* and the woman can't say anything without having it turned into a sexual leer. The problem is that usually she's trying to avoid rudeness herself, so she ends up frustrated and angry later on for letting him get away with it. It's like fending off an octopus.

The only way to handle this sort of leering boor is to stop talking altogether and walk away from him. If you can't do that, just say, "Well, I have to get back to work," and leave him standing in the puddle of his leering. There is nothing like a sudden shutout to put a person off balance. Even if the two of you are alone, it will embarrass him to be cut off in the middle of his lecherous banter. He will be less likely to put you through such an obnoxious ordeal again if he knows you will reject him. Since his whole purpose is to get you to accept him, and he has failed in no uncertain terms, he will eventually cool it and grow up. Or at least shut up, which is just as good.

Women who indulge in this type of behavior are somewhat easier to handle when they start leering with or about men. Women have the option to shut these women out of conversations and to exclude them from lunchtime gatherings. Men can challenge the woman by taking her propositions seriously and frightening her; since the psychology here is that the woman feels safe in making these insinuations in the office situation, removing that safeguard will throw her off balance and perhaps scare her into good manners.

The best way to handle such people is to shut them out from any personal interaction and limit your contact with them to times when it is necessary to deal with them about business. It probably won't do much good to tell them straight out that their remarks are having the reverse effect of their intentions, although it is fair to make a try. If it works, then you've solved the problem amicably; if not, silent rejection is the only other course of action.

ROVING EYES: WHEN THE OFFENDER IS YOUR BOSS

At times bosses may make remarks to their people that may come across as sexually oriented or offensive in some way. These remarks may be too personal, but because of daily interaction familiarity tips over into overfamiliarity. The boss may continually stare at his woman associate's blouse instead of maintaining eye contact. This can be unnerving, even if the boss is not aware he is doing it. Women may also do the same thing to men. Sometimes there is a real sexual curiosity, other times there isn't; either way it can make the person being viewed uncomfortable.

It is impossible to keep one's eyes away from all parts of a person; it is as uncomfortable to glare directly into someone's face for a whole meeting as to stare at her blouse. If you are an attractive person or dress particularly well, you must realize that people enjoy viewing something pleasing to the eye. It is also biologically normal behavior to examine a person who enters your office—even if it gets to the point of scrutiny, and even if the person comes in every day. This is part of our instinctive protective behavior. When the instinct graduates on to visually undressing someone, then the subject must be broached, or the matter handled subtly.

If your relationship with your boss is loose enough, you can make a joke about it. When your boss is staring at you intently, you might say, "Well, leave something on—I don't want to catch a cold." Such a light remark can offset embarrassment just because the matter has been brought into the open, in an inoffensive way. It relieves the sexual mystery, makes you more of a lighthearted than a mysterious figure, and removes the taboo that may have sparked the interest in the first place. There is nothing like a little sardonic wit to cool sexual ardor.

If you cannot do this, you might be a little more formal and say, "Excuse me, Mr. Jackson, did I lose your attention?" Or, if you want to be amusing but not sarcastic, you can wave your hand and say, "Earth to Boss . . . Earth to Boss."

If your boss periodically makes remarks about your appearance past the point of friendly compliments, you should either accept them with a bright "Thank you!", like Bette Davis getting an award; or, if you want to stop them, start to return each compliment or remark in kind. By doing this you can make this constant stream of remarks appear absurd, or make him as tired of your compliments as you are of his.

If he thinks your blouses are sexy, you can admire the hair on his arms. If he thinks you look tired and asks what you were doing the night before—tell him. Only tell him in such boring detail that it will kill his interest. If he thinks you need more makeup—or less makeup—ask him if he forgot to shave and closely scrutinize his jaw.

TO KILL A BOSS'S ARDOR

If your boss makes an overt pass at you, there is only one way to handle it, no matter how angry or offended you may be. Take it seriously and calmly, and point out that to follow through on such an act would make it impossible to work efficiently together. Also remind him that such things always get around the office and you could not deal with being a focus of gossip. Also suggest that you are not sure if you could look at him with the same respect as a business associate if you knew him intimately on a physical level.

This tactic was given to me by a woman whose boss did approach her during the first week she started working for him. "I was disgusted in the first place," she said, "but I wasn't about to let him know that. It was too good a job to lose. I couldn't believe that this egotistical reptile seriously thought I would go to bed with him if circumstances were different, but he believed it. And from that point on he never tried or even intimated he wanted to and we got along beautifully in the office."

This approach is good because it sidesteps the issue of personal rejection; it is based on a prudent business action, which even undiscriminating people can accept. For some people the idea that they could have had someone sexually is as good as the actual having—it is all an ego gratification. By rejecting the offer on a personal basis you place a wall around yourself that will only make the person want you more, or make him hate you for rejecting him. No matter what your true reaction is in a business situation, take the political rather than the emotional action whenever possible.

HARASSMENT

Sexual harassment involves a person using his or her position to obtain sexual favors from an employee. The implication is that one's job can either be improved or hampered depending on one's willingness to cooperate. Sexual harassment also involves going one step further, actually taking a real physical liberty with someone's body, whether it is a man fondling a woman in an intimate way or anyone placing anyone else in a compromising position. Asking an employee to go to dinner or to come into one's office for a private chat, or maneuvering someone into a hotel room, then actually pursuing the person for sex—this is sexual harassment. It was funny in *Sugar Babies;* in real life it becomes a matter for a lawsuit.

There is a distinction that must be made between finding out whether or not a co-worker would like to engage in sex and placing someone in a compromising position against his or her wishes. There is no doubt that some bosses are attractive to their employees and would find willing partners in the company. Commonly, bosses who harass do not care if the targets of their desires want to go to bed with them; they are after something else—ego gratification and a power trip that should be rejected.

Anyone who harasses anyone else sexually should be fired, or at least severely reprimanded, if possible. If the person is too high in the company, then the harassed person must decide either to file a lawsuit or leave the job, or both. There is no polite way to handle such a situation. It's like asking a rape victim to mind her manners.

In a large advertising agency several years back there was a young man who was hired in a capacity that allowed him access to the people who cast models for commercials. The person decided to use the company's name to get model agencies to send actors and models to his home for dinner and to see if they were "right" for a certain commercial. At dinner the models were then propositioned sexually. It didn't last long. When the agency people heard of it, they immediately complained and the man was fired.

HANDLING PASSES

Not all sexual overtures are done badly in an office situation, nor are all of them considered insulting. But most women feel that having to run an obstacle course of offers or insinuations is maddening. Offices seem to breed people who think mostly of sex, although in reality it just provides a handier place for such people to express their wishes. Boredom with the office routine and the daily interaction with people of the opposite sex brings many things to the fore.

The only way to make a pass to a co-worker is to arrange a private meeting away from the office, or a time when you won't be observed, then do it in a complimentary manner. Follow the basic guidelines of discretion; take time to get to know the person first and to ascertain if he or she would be attracted to you, and make the offer as an adult.

If you are interested in someone, take her/ him to lunch or invite her/ him for drinks after work—this is the best way. If the response is positive, you can go from the bar to the trysting place and not have to deal with second thoughts and embarrassed looks of anticipation in the office.

The way to turn down a pass should be in line with the way it is made. If the pass is sleazy, it should be put down hard. But be sure not to reject the person, just the manner in which the pass was made. If you would not be interested under any circumstances, say that you have a friend and explain no further. Don't prolong the situation by giving the person an opening to harass you because he feels rejected. Sleazy as he may have been, remember that it is best to be expedient, and forgo venting your anger or insulting the person. Think only in terms of a smooth relationship in the future.

If the pass is polite, but you aren't interested, just thank the person and say no. If you will never be interested, you can say you just do not have encounters with people you work with and leave it at that. And stay friends.

If you want to go to bed with the person, then take it from there. Don't be coy or play games, just suggest something, like drinks after work. Conduct it as much as possible out of the office.

OH, NO, NOT HIM!

What can be more of a jolt than to suddenly find yourself being introduced to a former one-night stand who comes to work in your office? It can be disconcerting, but remember that if this is the case, you are probably over twenty-one and should have some sort of maturity in these matters.

The best thing is not to refer to the actual sex, but not to pretend that you never saw the person before. People hate being forgotten as sexual partners more than anything. Just be friendly and continue with the person as if he or she has some basis for conversation with you. You can say you met once before and take that as a start for a good future working relationship. Don't get into a high-school kid's bag of what if he still wants to. Chances are he doesn't. If the person has been persistent and you know he *does* want to, then be very friendly and crisp and businesslike. And next time he calls say you just don't make it with people you work with—even if you did once before. You can also say that sort of thing is frowned on in the company (you were there first, right?) and you knew people to be denied advancement because of rumors. . . .

THE SECRET STORM

It is useless to deny that actual sexual encounters are carried out in the privacy—or hoped-for privacy—of offices, Xerox rooms, file rooms, wherever two people can convince themselves they will not be discovered. Wherever there is an executive office with a couch, it is pretty likely that if the couch could speak it would not bore you with its stories. It is best not to engage in sex in the office, however. The problem of etiquette arises when someone walks in on a sexual tryst by accident. The "tryst" may encompass anything from some heavy kissing to actual intercourse. Who is the one to make apologies—the sexual participants or the person who entered without knocking?

If you are rude enough to enter any office without knocking—even if the occupant is alone and working—then you are most surely in the wrong. The only thing you can do is say you are sorry and clear out quickly. After that, either keep totally quiet about the incident, or, if asked, assure the couple that their secret is safe. And keep it safe.

If you have been discovered in the act of serious sex by your boss, you are truly at his mercy. It is grounds for dismissal, although it is doubtful that any competent employer would take this action against productive employees. Whether or not in-office hanky-panky alone is cause for dismissal lies solely with the employer. The most sensible course of action would be to reprimand the people involved and warn against future in-office interaction of this sort. If you are discovered in an embrace, it is not fair grounds for dismissal, and you should challenge such a decision if it is made. It is not proper to engage in any sort of romantic activity in the office, but one should still not expect such a drastic retribution for making what is basically an acceptable error in judgment that need not be repeated.

If you regularly engage in sex in the office and you are a high enough officer in the company, your trysts should be conducted when your co-workers are not around, such as after hours or before hours. For many superbusy executives, the office may be the only feasible place to have sex in many cases. If this is so, try to arrange something so that you will not be offending anyone else's sensibilities. Because of the nature of perks for executives, it may even be possible to arrange some sort of understanding that you require such a place and can make use of the company apartment, or obtain an allowance to maintain a trysting place near the office. These days it is up to the company to decide what is useful to executive efficiency, despite what may be considered a breach in morals or good taste.

If you are discovered by anyone in the act of love in any place that is not normally private, it is up to you to apologize to the person who discovered you. A person should reasonably expect to enter the company library and not have to check for bodies first.

The best course of action between co-workers who share a secret of this kind is to play it down: an apology if the discovery is undeniably *flagrante;* a tacit assumption of innocence if the scene was ambiguous enough to pretend that something else was going on.

If someone walks in on a tryst well into its final stages and, not expecting to find two bodies on the floor, screams before she thinks, then the situation enters the realm of farce. It will be impossible to maintain discretion, since a scream in an office will bring other concerned parties to the rescue. In such a case, quickly get your clothes in order and make up some fast excuse and hope that it is believed—or that everyone will pretend it didn't happen. Don't discuss it any further unless you are called on it by the boss. In this case you can either deny it or hope you are too valuable an employee to be fired.

GUILT WITHOUT SEX

There are times when people may be alone together in an office doing something that is not sexual, but are discovered by someone who thinks it is. One of these things is back rubbing. One office I know has a person who likes to rub women's backs. It is stated that this man has no sexual interest in doing this; further, the women—or some of them—enjoy the free massage. If this is done publicly, it runs into the problem of causing some sort of discomfort to people who are bothered by intimate contact of any sort in an office situation. If done behind closed doors, the discomfort takes on the shape of a mild titillation.

It should always be remembered that extensive touching—especially between the sexes—always looks funny in the office. For one thing, it is difficult to believe that a man who likes to rub women's backs is not obtaining some sort of subliminal sexual gratification—if only psychologically. This does not necessarily make it wrong, since people have been known to receive subliminal sexual gratification watching girls get on and off the bus; in this case office policy and the acceptance of offbeat behavior by co-workers is the decisive factor.

If a guideline is asked for, it should be ascertained if the person is in fact improving office morale or degrading it. Psychologists would probably say that letting this human, harmless pleasantry continue would be preferable to making an arbitrary decison against it based on militant etiquette.

VARIETIES
Gay Kids Like Privacy, Too

Gay people are much more accepted in business and by corporations today than before. Even conservative companies in the Midwest will no longer fire someone because of homosexuality. One company I know that doesn't allow men to have beards or wear anything other than a suit and tie at any time also has in its code the statement that an employee may not be fired for being gay. The person may not move up in the company easily, but his job is safe as long as he maintains the corporate image and does his job.

Being gay in an office should not be an end all in itself. There is no more reason to discuss your life-style with co-workers than there is for heterosexual people to flaunt their affairs. Always remember that the basic thing that makes a person gay is the fact of what he or she likes to do in bed. That's the heart of the matter, and there isn't much reason to get into that in an office.

If you think someone you work with is gay but this person has not imparted the information, it is rude to ask out of curiosity. I once heard a secretary ask a person point-blank in the middle of a three-way conversation, "Are you gay?" The girl she asked just said, "At times I am, but it makes me sad to hear a question like that." Any kind of superpersonal question is out of order. Questions probing a person's sex preference, sex life, or related activities are particularly rude.

If you do have a sex-related distinction that could conceivably cause problems on the job, you should make it known to your employer. Just being homosexual is not one of these things. But if you plan to have your lover accompany you to company-related affairs, then you are declaring yourself publicly and your employer should be informed.

We were told of one bank teller who on his third day of work showed up fully dressed in female attire. He wasn't gay, but he was a cross-dresser. He had not given any indication of this when applying for the job and on his first three days dressed impeccably in suit and tie. Surprisingly, the bank did not fire him; they just insisted that he pick a side and dress that way all the time. Since he did not feel he could work under those conditions, he quit, proving only that the true stories in business are more fantastic than anything one could make up.

Unmarried Couples

Today there is nothing unusual about a man and a woman living together without being married, but some conservative companies might still disapprove. It is not a point of etiquette to obtain your employer's approval of your choice of living arrangements, but if you have the kind of job that can be affected by your personal life, it is best to make it known that they exist—or to maintain an air of total secrecy.

BOSS'S WIFE AND KIDS

What happens when the boss's wife or a member of his family makes a pass? It is really difficult, and the only thing to do is turn it down and hope for the best. Even an innocent employee may be fired if the wife decides to say he made a pass at her. If the boss's wife is known for this behavior, and you feel the information may be well received, you might find some way to let your boss know. The situation is always risky. If you do get fired and you know this is the reason, discuss it with someone else high up in the company, such as the personnel director, or someone who is close to the boss and hope for the best. Don't tell him yourself unless you feel he will be fair. But remember, he probably already knows and won't want you around even if you're innocent.

If the boss decides you are right for his little girl, give him the chance, and if you don't want to get involved with the person, assume that it was a social invitation and let them have the impression you are already spoken for.

THE LITTLE WOMAN

It happens that in American business today old-fashioned mores are often superimposed on current life-styles. Two friends of mine are in partnership together. An invitation to attend a gala at the British Embassy in Washington was sent to one of them, at the office. The invitation was for him and his wife. Since he was not married he called back personally to RSVP and told the man who handled the call that he was not married and asked if he could bring his partner instead. The man became very distressed and said that everyone would be in couples since it was a dinner and dance. My friend said that in that case he would bring a woman friend, and that he had assumed it was a business invitation, which was why he had asked.

The other man suddenly became very cold and strange and said, "I'm sorry, but we will have to cancel your invitation—there won't be enough room for a guest." My friend asked why they had sent an invitation for two people if there was only room for one; and the man canceled the whole invitation altogether. This very strange occurrence brings forth the whole question of presupposing that everyone is married—or else. In an embassy situation, of course, people are so circumspect that they will go to great lengths to avoid politically unappetizing situations—such as an unmarried couple, or two men attending a party together—and will resort to outright rudeness to avoid them.

The insulted party had no real outlet for this outrage except to write to the ambassador and demand an apology, but then he figured the person who did the offending would probably intercept it. It's best to let such a situation go by the board, since no real personal or business damage was done.

THE MARRIEDS

It is not common that two people who are married will work as employees in a company. It is more common that they will own the company. If they do, it is their responsibility to make sure they do not place any of their employees in a position of having to take sides between them. One friend of mine noted that he worked for a married couple and found himself having to smile embarrassedly a lot because of their squabbles in the office. "I was often criticized by Stu for doing better work for Paula, or by Paula for taking sides with Stu because he was a man."

By the same token, one half of a married couple should not act like someone's mama when things are going rough between Stu and another employee, or act like papa just because it seems that everyone should be part of his and Paula's family. Warm business relationships are one thing; but placing people in the position of being your kids and relatives doesn't work. Treat employees like employees, and respect them as human beings who may move on to other jobs eventually.

PROMOTING YOUR LOVER

It happens in the business world that lovers are often connected in strange ways to business. You may be a writer whose lover is building a career as an architect, and by writing about his work in stories where appropriate, you can help promote his or her career. There is in fact nothing wrong with this unless every story you write includes your lover's work. To promote one's lover is perfectly acceptable if that person is talented and can do the job as well as a stranger. Most business advancement is due to the personal relationships you can build anyway.

People would not hesitate to help advance a friend, yet they may be leery of helping a spouse or lover who is also worthwhile. One should avoid promoting a lover if someone else deserves it more and has first choice on the advancement. Never push aside a worthy person to advance your lover, but don't leave your lover to flounder if you can help.

JUICY MORSELS

Gossip about people's romantic affairs is strictly taboo, just as is any gossip that may bring harm to a person's career. Since this is the most dangerous gossip of all in a business situation, it is to be avoided totally. It is not anyone's place to pass judgment on the morality of a co-worker, a boss, or an employee as long as the affair is kept discreet and does not affect the survival of the company or affect anyone's career. Because sexual gossip tends to be erroneous, since no one usually can have a firsthand account, there is an additional reason for remaining silent on the subject. We covered gossip in another section of this book, but since this area is so sensitive and prone to so much falsehood and sensationalism, it is important to point up the need to steer away from it.

PUPPY LOVE

Though it seems unimportant to most people, harmless crushes are a nice part of the lighter side of romantic attractions in the office. A teenage mailroom boy who starts sending flowers and cards to the pretty secretary five years older than he is not someone who should be put down, although some insensitive people may do so. These occurrences add something to the atmosphere that reminds us that at the base of sexual attraction are the freshness and innocence that set our adult tastes. If this charming romantic aspect can be kept alive instead of trampled, perhaps there will be fewer people who present the sleazy side of the sexual coin when they grow up.

Most people like romanticism; it helps the soul to remember the callow poetry and high-mindedness that characterize schoolboy crushes. Without belaboring the point further, if someone of any age puts a single rose on your desk, don't crush it under a pile of work.

6

A GOOD "GIRL" IS HARD TO FIND

IT'S BEST TO make it clear at the start that it is bad manners to refer to any woman in business as "girl," no matter what her age. The fact that people do refer to their female secretaries in that condescending way is part of the reason why we need guidelines for etiquette in relating to secretaries. It is also no longer correct to think of secretaries as being strictly female, since so many men are again occupying these jobs. The very title of the job has developed an almost pejorative meaning. Many talented, valuable people don't like to admit that they are secretaries. Many companies have shifted the job title to "assistant," thus blurring the appellation as well as the stigma.

Secretaries are essential to business. No company can function without them. There is probably no other person in an office whose absence can so effectively cripple the daily routine. Yet secretaries are belittled by the people they work for, taken for granted, treated as menials, paid lower-scale salaries, and asked to do all sorts of things not included in the job title. There is a shortage of secretaries—especially good secretaries—and it's easy to see why.

Some secretaries are treated with careless manners, others may be bad-mannered themselves. There are also instances where the secretary and her boss get along wonderfully and have relationships based on mutual respect, understanding, and consideration.

THE RIGHT START

It is part of the consideration due any new secretary to set forth your expectations of her duties before the first day on the job. If you start off allowing the secretary to act like a princess royal or to be sloppy about the work, she will be correct in assuming that's the way the job is and you'll never be able to get on the right track.

The secretary must also be definitive. If she starts off picking up the dry cleaning, shopping for members of the boss's family, and doing any number of personal tasks just to get off on the right foot, then she can't regret having to maintain those duties forever. If she was willing to run errands on her lunch hour the first week, it is only logical for her boss to assume that she won't mind doing it regularly.

"I DON'T DO WINDOWS"

Set your limits at the start. Too many secretaries are afraid to be professional in voicing their expectations at interviews because they are afraid of not getting the job. Before going into the interview, make a list of things you don't want to do and state them to your prospective employer. If some personal duties are required, make your compromises as you see fit and stick to them politely, but stick to them.

If things are made clear right at the beginning, there should be no problems later on. There are, of course, basic secretarial duties that are part of every job. There are specialties of the house that any boss will want. The secretary should discuss them with the boss before accepting the job. Because there is getting to be a shortage of competent secretaries, since many women tend not to want to get into this line of work anymore and not enough men are opting for it, a secretary has somewhat more clout these days than she did previously. But he or she should always remember that a secretary's job by its nature is somewhat open-ended and freely interpreted by the boss.

Things to be made clear at the start involve these areas:

Coffee making: Is the secretary expected to make and serve coffee as part of her routine? Does the boss do it if her schedule is upset? One private secretary who has worked for men, and now has a woman boss, says that the men never will take on this job, but it's shared with her female boss.

Family affairs: Does the boss or boss's wife expect to have the secretary make her plans for her and do her shopping? One private secretary felt very used by the boss's wife. "Fran would call and say, 'Dear, can you make reservations for us at the Four Seasons? . . . Then, dear, can you go to Saks and pick up something for me?'

"I resented it mostly because she'd couch it in those terms of sweetness, and also because I had work to do and I knew she had nothing to do at home except go shopping.

"I also got what I may have projected as a superior attitude from their daughter, who I felt condescended to me as a menial, when we were the same age and had the same education. But because her mother treated me like a servant, she had a low opinion of me and it showed when she talked to me."

Clearly, a private secretary can't avoid encounters with her boss's family, but it should be made clear at the start who the secretary is working for. Many secretaries are college educated and do not want to do errands.

Personal affairs: Many private secretaries do their boss's banking for them. This kind of errand is usually considered part of the job for the simple reason that it takes so long to stand in line at a bank, and the boss has a right to ask his secretary to do it as part of her duties. Most secretaries do not mind shopping for the boss when asked in the proper way. "My boss tells me to go get a present for his wife, and I resent it. I don't know what his wife wants, and I think he should ask me if I'd mind doing it." Another secretary, who worked for a woman, says, "I don't mind doing it, because she would do it for me if I was busy. When she goes out she always says, 'I'm going to stop at the drugstore, do you need anything?' It's more of a give-and-take and I'm only returning the favor. I feel like a professional, not an employee, with her."

SAY "PLEASE," PLEASE

A favor asked of a secretary should be requested with the same politeness you would ask anyone to do something special for you. A secretary may not feel that the request can ever be refused, but a boss should always ask first if it would be an imposition, then make the request, even if the favor is being done on company time. Always let your secretary know that you see her as a professional working person, not as someone who can be turned on and off with buttons.

One top executive we interviewed said that his secretary will say to him at times, "Richard, say 'please.'" He takes this in the manner it is given, since she knows that any seeming rudeness to her is an indication that he is tense or harassed or in a bad mood, which may also cause him to be short with an important client. "She knows I'm not actually meaning to be rude to her, and her reprimand is a protection of me."

The problem that arises in any business relationship—and especially between boss and secretary—is that of familiarity. A secretary is so much a part of the fabric of the job that the boss forgets she is not truly attached to his shoulder like an arm and starts using her as an extension of himself. "A good secretary is truly your best friend," one exec told me, "and you have to treat her as someone very special."

Because of this special relationship that may or may not develop, despite the formality or informality of it, the ground rules should be established at the start. If you expect a girl Friday, then get off to that at the start. If you want a strictly formal, business relationship, with a very clear line between personal and office life, make that clear too.

SMALL EXPECTATIONS

There are two kinds of secretaries: the private secretary whose job is so closely aligned with her boss's that she could conceivably take over his job better than anyone else if the need arose; and the "girl" in the general secretary pool who reports to an office manager and who takes assignments from more than one person.

Oddly enough, the complaints from both are similar. There is something about a woman behind a typewriter that brings out the crudeness in a man. She is seen as being as much a machine as the object she's typing letters on. She often ends by doing her work under a cloud of tense resentment because of the way she was asked to do the typing in the first place.

Most complaints from secretaries revolve around the way they are asked—or ordered—to do a job. A boss may walk up to her, disregarding whatever else she may be doing, and start telling her what he wants done. She may be on the phone or typing already. There is no "Excuse me" or "Will you . . ." to preface the instructions, just a bunch of papers placed on the desk and fast instructions barked out. Nobody should have to work under those conditions.

"People always assume that when I'm on the phone, it's a personal call," one secretary told me. "They interrupt or talk to me while I'm on the phone, making it difficult to hear the caller."

Another secretary works for a woman who rents a suite in a legal firm. "Once I was on the phone with a client and one of the lawyers from the firm looked in and waved some papers at me. Of course, I ignored him. He came back in a few seconds later and said, 'Are you still on the phone? I have some typing for you!'

"I asked my caller to hold and snapped at the lawyer, 'I don't work for your company!' and went back to my call."

Other complaints are based on the expectation that a secretary is goofing off if she leaves her desk for the women's room or to take a drink of water. "They treat us like nonentities," said one secretary who works in a pool. "I'm thought of not as a person but as a fixture at the desk."

Some secretaries complain about the depersonalization that occurs when a boss says, "Have your girl call my girl," rather than refer to her in more professional terms, such as "my secretary." In an office pool the reference is always to a "she," not to a person with a name, which is irksome to secretaries.

Personal needs of secretaries—especially, they say, secretaries who work for men—are never considered. "If I need to leave early to have a dentist's appointment the men will scream about it," says a secretary in a pool. "Most of us are afraid to leave even fifteen minutes early, but everyone else may take hours off for the same reason. It's as if we don't have to go to doctors or have any of the private needs that other people in the office have."

THE RIGHT WAY

Secretaries would like these amenities observed:

- Refer to them by their names or titles when asking for them.
- Observe some form of politeness when asking them to perform their duties, even though the duty is part of the job. "Please" and "Thank you" go a long way here and get better results and a willingness to do the extras that make office life easier.
- If the secretary is superbusy or on the phone, either wait a few minutes or let her know that you're aware of her dither before talking. "When you have the time" or "When you are free . . ." is the politeness here.
- Don't make a blanket assumption that the secretary is on a personal call when she's on the phone, or that she is goofing off when she goes to the rest room. Save your macho man act for the swingers' club and don't start bad-mouthing her for

laziness just because she isn't at her desk. Everyone gets thirsty.

- If you share a secretary, don't put her in the middle of a tug-of-war. She is there to work for several people, but she can only serve one set of typewritten copies at a time. Provide her with a range of time to do the job, and trust her to do it as soon as she can. If you need a rush job, ask the previous executive if she can put his aside, rather than threatening or cozying up to her to do it. Don't insult her by putting her in a bad position with her other bosses.

- If she needs to leave early and if it's possible, ask her if that is enough time or whether she needs more. This small politeness will earn greater loyalty and more willingness to expend more effort for you when you're in need.

- Make her feel good about being a secretary by telling her when she does a good job instead of assuming that she's a lazy, dumb little bimbo just because she works in a typing pool.

PRIVATE LIVES

Between a boss and his secretary there are no real secrets—the secretary knows all about you, despite her discretion. If she doesn't, she probably isn't that good a secretary. No matter how badly the rest of the world thinks of you, it's important that your secretary be loyal, since she is the one who can most assuredly protect you or discredit you.

One of the crudest men I ever met in a top executive position had a string of the best and happiest secretaries I ever saw. Part of it was because he viewed them as intelligent professionals, dealt with them in a clear-cut, businesslike way, and expected them to know their job without his patronizing them in any way. I talked to one of his secretaries, and she said that he was the best male boss she ever had. He was never rude to her, never asked her to do anything that was out of her frame of reference, respected the fact that she wasn't always at the desk, and always informed her of his whereabouts and how long he'd be anywhere.

He was, in fact, predictable, so she knew clearly where she stood. Others might have run into an unexpected tirade of rudeness or rage from him, but he never abused his secretary. They were on a first-name basis; he gave her a gift each Christmas and said "Happy birthday" when it was time. And he let her do her job.

This is probably the ideal for any secretary. But some do become closer to their bosses and strong ties of friendship come to cement their loyalties. One friend of mine has a secretary who knows exactly how her boss thinks. She is formal and polite on the phone until she finds out if you are friend or business. If she can handle the business herself—such as making an appointment—she does so. If not and he is available, she will pass the call in to him, first briefing him on who the caller is and what he wants. Eleanor never barricades calls, but she makes sure that his workday is not thrown out of kilter by calls he can't handle immediately. Personal calls are heavily screened on busy days, and friends are told when to call back.

In some ways this is taking a lot on herself, but she is only working the way he told her to. She also is close friends with him and his wife. She keeps a judicious distance when it's time, and joins in when she knows she can. She is familiar but professional, and never is pushy or contemptuous.

"MY FRIEND, MY SECRETARY"

It's a rare thing to find someone who can be a close personal friend as well as an efficient secretary. Sometimes the mix can lead to sloppiness or taking too much on, or to the inevitable firing of a friend. One must be supercareful when to take down the barrier between personal and office lives.

One executive says he depends totally on his secretary, talks to her as a friend, but maintains a line between what he does at home and what he does in the office. "She knows better than I do who I should talk to when they call at the office," he says, "but I do not let this friendship pass out of the office. She doesn't expect it or want it and neither do I." People can have strong, affectionate, and intimate relationships with each other in some situations, but they may be extremely awkward in others.

It is not usual that someone making $100,000 a year and socializing in places with people of that financial level will be able to socialize with his or her secretary, except on special occasions, no matter how much they love each other. Other people, however, who do not lead a jet-powered life, no matter what their income, and keep a "nice mix" of friends, usually can find much to share with secretaries on the home front.

A lawyer and his secretary would have much in common because of the basic similarity of interests and intelligence. Because some secretaries have been able to move into high executive slots and there is no longer the idea that a secretary must stay a secretary, the social lines that have existed are weaker than before.

The determining factor is how well your secretary fits in with your personal social setup, and whether you and the secretary want to spend that much time together. The whole etiquette of making any friends from the office is based on preferences and nothing else.

SETTING LIMITS

It is possible to get too personal with your boss or secretary even if you do not share any of your personal social life. A secretary almost cannot help knowing a boss's secrets, because it is impossible to be totally discreet in an office. A secretary knows at least the names of a boss's friends. At least twice I have been introduced to women socially who, on hearing my name, knew all about me because they were secretaries of friends of mine. It is polite for any secretary to maintain her knowledge in silence, rather than display the fact that she is privy to surprising knowledge about the people she works for. If a secretary knows anything personal, it is part of her professional courtesy to forget it.

Bosses who have secretaries who are contemporaries in age often develop friendships with them, and later both may wish to extricate themselves from the personal part of the interaction. It is best to set limits at the start. Early enthusiasms of friendship commonly die down. The thing to remember about any personal/ business relationship is that both sides usually maintain the same sentiments at the same time. Just because you spent several months having dinner, going to shows, and running around together does not mean you can't cool off the social part of the relationship at a certain point and maintain a warm working situation. The way to do it is to stop making so many dates; beg off on some invitations; phase out some or most of the get-togethers.

ANGER AND RESENTMENT

More perhaps than any other working relationship, that of boss and secretary is most likely to incite the kind of anger and underlying resentments common in personal relationships. Just as with personal interactions, it is necessary to the health of the working situation to keep avenues of communication open. If there are problems or objections felt by either the secretary or the boss, they should be aired before they become gnawing resentments. It must also be remembered that this is a business relationship and objections should not be made on a personal level. If the secretary chews gum, the boss must couch his objections in professional terms: "I do not want the image that gum chewing represents in my office." It is not acceptable to say, "You look and sound like a teenybopper, so put the gum in the wastebasket or I'll put it on your nose."

It may be somewhat more difficult for a secretary to present objections to the boss, but the door must be left open for this eventuality, otherwise the secretary's resentment may be based on the fact that there is no avenue of complaint. A shared secretary may have many more resentments than a private secretary, since there are so many more "bosses" to deal with. It is unfortunate that these pool secretaries often are used badly and rudely and don't have any avenue of complaint since there is no one head of the place and their executives don't rely on just one secretary. In such a case the secretary should deal directly with the offending executive; or, if this person has caused resentments with all the secretaries, they should make a united complaint at the same time directly to the person. The same holds true in reverse, from exec to secretary.

The problem for pool secretaries is that they are not really in any position to set limits. They can refuse to do personal things for executives, but they can't stop the requests. The unfortunate thing is that many good secretaries become turned off with the job itself and go into other lines of work, rather than seeking better secretarial positions.

LOVE LIVES

Sometimes male executives feel it is part of their successful images to have mistresses as well as wives. Female executives may also carry on various affairs. We knew of one very famous woman entrepreneur who had a paid masseur come in daily for a massage and/or sex. She also had a husband, but the physical part of their marriage was over, and she relied on him for emotional and psychological support.

When a secretary must cover for a boss's sexual affairs, it is usually the case of a male boss hiding the fact of his affair or affairs from his wife. Women execs may do the same thing, but they are less likely to expect anyone else to cover for them. Whatever the actual situation, the etiquette is still the same. The boss must provide the stated excuse for the secretary to provide to the spouse, or whoever it is for; and the secretary is not to be considered privy to the true facts. The less a secretary knows, the better off everyone will be.

No boss should ever ask a secretary to lie for him or her. This is rude, and it places the secretary in a compromising position, especially if the situation should ever end up in court. The rule should apply to any matter, not just romance. It is all right for a secretary to say you can't come to a phone when you can't, but in matters of legality, the secretary has a right to be exempt from implication.

"I'M A SECRETARY, NOT A PUMP"

Husbands and wives should never pump secretaries, but they do. Secretaries should always ask the boss what to say if someone calls, so at least the stories will jibe. If a caller continues to pump, the secretary should say there is another call coming in and she will call back. Usually the wife will say, "Never mind," and let the secretary go. If she persists, the secretary should say that she is being called away by someone in the office.

It is never the secretary's job to judge the morality of her boss's behavior, sexual or otherwise, unless his actions will implicate her in an illegal act. If a boss wants to carry on extramaritally, then he also should handle all the lies and cover-ups required. Tell the secretary what to say and when, then stick with it. Don't leave the excuses to her imagination.

GIFTS

No matter how efficient your secretary is, you should not lose sight of the fact that efficiency is part of the job. If she is a star at this aspect, then you may want to make it known to her that you recognize and appreciate it. Unfortunately, some bosses overplay it. One friend told us about his secretary, who was so good and did so much out of love that he got into the bad policy of giving her expensive Christmas presents, birthday gifts, and such. The secretary, who was basically only doing what she felt was her job and who felt her boss had given her so much in the way of kindness and moral support, started trying to reciprocate by matching the cost of the gifts. It became a viciously expensive spiral—especially for the secretary.

Christmas is definitely the time to tell your secretary you appreciate her. It is also a time to make sure she does not give you a gift in return, except some token thing. Make it clear that your gift is not for Christmas but to express thanks.

A gift costing fifty dollars would be considered generous at any level. More than that is going overboard, even in a place where the secretary is the only other person in the office. The company may also give a bonus at this time, but that is separate from your personal gift.

The gift itself can be some article of clothing such as a sweater or scarf, a handbag (but not shoes), or—probably most preferably—a gift certificate at her favorite store. We only mention wearables to note that it is appropriate for a male boss to give a female secretary something to wear, as long as it's not underclothing and is a "neutral" enough article that it does not conflict with her personal style. For example, sweaters, vests, scarves, or hats may be appropriate, whereas skirts, slacks, or dresses are not. It points up the lack of intimate involvement between her and the boss, while adding a somewhat familial warmth to the gift. Besides, his wife may have chosen it, which is even better.

Birthdays are best remembered with flowers or candy or, as one secretary said, "the best thing—a single rose." An invitation to lunch is also very good, and if you can afford it, give her the day off. This is not an outrageous policy; some companies have it as part of their employee benefits. Secretaries do not think it is necessary to receive birthday gifts at all, and everyone agrees it is not in good taste or good policy to give them.

One executive always brings a gift back for his secretary—as well as for others on the staff—when he goes to a foreign country on company business. His business is with a nonprofit cultural organization, so he is actually sharing with the workers a form of freebie. It is nice, however, to remember a secretary on your travels with some interesting gift from the place you visit.

Many people in the office who have the secretary's services available remember her in a special way by bringing flowers to her periodically for her desk. One man we knew made a policy of bringing a single, special flower every Monday to the secretary. It never became expected, but it was a regular "nice" thing that everyone in the office looked forward to.

Probably the best thing people can do for any harassed secretary is to ask if they can get anything for her during the day when they go out. Secretaries can seldom spare time to get to the store for the kind of shopping most others do on lunch hours, and this kind of thoughtfulness is always appropriate from anyone, executive or co-secretary or boss.

Some bosses will do something like having their own Xerox copies made when the secretary is superbusy, and this takes the form of being a kind of gift. It is the thoughtfulness, not the actual gift, that the secretary appreciates.

Gifts for a secretary should go along these lines:

First year: perfume, or some small wearable, about fifteen dollars.

Second year: leather, such as a bag, around fifty dollars.

Third year: gift certificate, same price.

Five or more: you can go up to a hundred dollars, but remember that you will be setting a standard to be kept up in future years. It is best to maintain a top of fifty dollars for gifts.

As for reciprocation, a secretary can give a small token gift to the boss, but it is not expected or necessary. The implication of a gift in business is that some special service beyond the call of duty has been performed and will continue to be. Since the boss doesn't provide this kind of service to the secretary, a gift isn't appropriate. If the secretary does want to express special feeling or appreciation to a well-liked boss, the gift should be small—a book, or a wallet, or a wearable accessory—and not exceed a small outlay of cash, in keeping with the secretary's salary.

PERSONAL PROBLEMS

In a secretary/boss relationship, the boss must extend some consideration to the secretary's human needs. It is not necessary for the boss to listen to his secretary's problems, no matter how good she is. Remember that being a secretary requires a certain amount of personal involvement—on a one-way basis.

The best approach is to provide your secretary with the leeway she needs, when she needs it, to handle personal affairs. Sometimes a divorce is in the offing, and she may need some time to be by herself. An offer to use temporary help here and there is worth it to keep a good secretary. In any event, provide that kind of consideration and state your moral support to her during times of stress. It is not polite to go much further than that.

BOYS AND GIRLS

A lovely woman friend of mine owns a small successful business, composed of a staff of herself and two younger men, one of them her secretary/assistant. Because there were two males in the office, she had been heard to refer to them as "the boys" when talking on the phone. Since no grown man likes being referred to as a boy in a business situation, the affectionate term rankled. It was solved subtly, without confrontation, when they gave her a card on an anniversary and signed it "The Boys," heavily underlined.

Even if you are in your fifties and your secretary is nineteen, you must give him or her the respect due to any person working in a professional business capacity. Secretaries might refer to themselves as girls among themselves, but that is a social term, and a familiar one. Never say to a business associate, "Have your girl call my girl." Never refer to any business associate on staff as a boy or girl, or guy or gal, unless the situation is informal enough to permit it. In any business situation always refer to a person by his or her name or position.

For example: "Have your secretary call my secretary"
or
"Have your secretary call Miss Johnson here at my office."

In the latter example, using your secretary's name will imply that her position is secretary or assistant.

If you have a male secretary, it is best to make sure that you say his name and indicate that he is your secretary, since most people do not yet expect a man when they call a secretary.

If a secretary only identifies herself by her first name (and most secretaries—at least female secretaries—do) then it is all right to ask for her or him by that name only. I always feel it is good to ask the person's whole name just in case you ever need to send something through the mail to the secretary's attention; it also indicates that you realize you are dealing with a person and not a machine named Ruth..

CALL ME MISTER

If you call a particular person often, his secretary may get on a first-name basis with you. This is not rude in most cases. There are some executives who will always have a strictly professional interaction and must always be called Mr. or Ms. Somebody. The relationships that allow first names to be used are usually established by the caller giving his first name without the last to the secretary. If you want to be called "Mr." or "Ms." or "Miss" or "Mrs.," then always identify yourself as such. This etiquette holds even between secretaries themselves.

ONE-SIDED ETIQUETTE

I always looked forward to calling my friend Tom at work because his secretary was such a delightful person on the phone. She was warm and friendly and could tell you that Tom was busy, in a meeting, or out in a way that was just right, and very businesslike, too. She remembered who I was from the first time I called, and after a few times she would say, "Hello, George," before I gave my name, because she recognized my voice.

So I was surprised when I told him once what a great secretary she was and he looked glum. I suggested he didn't know his own luck. He then told me that he had had many complaints about her because she was "flip" with the people in the office. No one liked her, and her rudeness toward them had gone so far that they complained to him about it.

His way of handling it was very good. He called her in and told her that she had received nothing but compliments from outsiders, but that her job also included being polite to the people she worked with every day. The problem, as Tom saw it, was that in her early working days she had worked not as a secretary but in a factory, and she didn't know that the politeness she was reserving for special people was something everyone had a right to expect.

Because she was a bright person and had no true inner hostility—she thought that politeness was a sometime thing—she changed and made an effort to turn things around. It worked. It always does. People in the office reversed their animosity and she became extremely well liked among the staff, as well as the perfect secretary for clients and bigwigs.

Anyone who presents negativity to his or her co-workers need not think that it is ever too late to change. People in offices never have a large stake in holding a grudge, and because office life is essentially boring, they are always happy to make room for anyone who wants to be nice.

GUARDIAN SECRETARY

Secretaries are often placed in the position of having to cover for the boss, making excuses, and getting rid of time wasters politely. The secretary is the middleman and the wailing wall. People who call may be rude to the secretary about her boss, then never express any sort of displeasure to the source of their hostility.

One owner of a small company told me that it was amusing to him because he and his secretary are very close and she protects him. Whenever such a person comes to the office, the secretary has a code by which she lets the owner know whether the visitor has been rude or polite. If a confrontation arises on another matter, the owner may pull the fact out of the blue and use it as a surprise tactic on the rude visitor. He also will be less likely to do business with a rude salesman if there are doubts on other levels as well.

Most secretaries see handling rudeness from callers as part of the job, and a good secretary will not waste energy fighting back. Because he or she is not involved, it is seen as part of the other person's problem and is not taken personally. There's more on this subject in chapter 8, "A Call Is Waiting."

It is not considered rude to have your secretary deal with people on the phone, to screen out those you can't talk to, or to delay certain callers.

It is also usually part of the secretary's job to decide what excuses to make. Hopefully, the secretary will not insult the caller's intelligence with transparent lies, but will use a repertoire of lines based on the accurate situation. There is nothing wrong with telling a caller that the boss is unavailable because of a meeting or that he or she is unable to take any calls at that time. It is honest, and everyone has a right to privacy or to be left alone during the workday. A caller should not be told that the person is in a meeting, then be put on hold, only to have the secretary come back and put the call through because the boss approved. It is better to take a number and call back to avoid looking like a liar.

It is also a common practice for a boss to tell the secretary to send a nice thank-you note to someone. Obviously this is the case of the superefficient secretary who really knows her boss's business as well as or better than he does. Since people reveal more to secretaries than to their bosses, very often the secretary may actually know better what to say to the person receiving the thank-you. People who maintain long business relationships do get to know an associate's secretary very well and form separate minifriendships of their own. It is a good idea to make friends with a secretary if you do business often with her boss, since she can expedite matters when things become rushed.

IMAGE AND SELF-IMAGE

Secretaries often can build up resentments, even when they are genuinely happy with their situations. One general area of dissatisfaction is being called secretaries when they are actually assistants who also perform secretarial duties.

Male secretaries resent it when callers ask to speak to "your female receptionist or secretary, please."

Secretaries may resent doing mop-ups when there is not adequate maid service. Others prefer to clean their own area, feeling that this is the only way it will be done properly.

Some resent dress codes that presume to tell them which colors or patterns are appropriate, or what hairstyles. Others resent having to dress up for work when the office is not cleaned properly.

Some secretaries find it troublesome having to deal on a one-to-one basis when it comes time to try to get raises. Others resent being automatically eliminated from consideration for advancement to other positions. They also resent there being more or less of a ceiling on the amount of money they can make as secretaries; they feel that incomes should reflect the importance of their bosses.

Many executives, especially male executives, as we mentioned earlier, treat secretaries as lower forms of office life, viewing them as anything from sexual robots to brainless machines. Too many secretaries accept something resembling a low self-image based on the fact that they are at the foundation, so to speak, of business life.

Etiquette begins at home, and with one's respect for oneself. A secretary should neither view his or her job as lowly nor be ashamed of the title. Any secretary who has rearranged the files before leaving a job knows how vital this job is to the functioning of a company. A secretary can save or cost a lot of money, enhance or destroy efficiency, save or destroy a reputation.

It is important to approach yourself as a professional, to project the idea that you deserve the same respect for your job as is expected from you. This rule is essential to dealing successfully in business. If a secretary does not know what he or she should expect in the way of fair and equal treatment, there is not much he or she can do to cue others.

RECEPTIONISTS
The Greeting Area

A receptionist conveys the first impression a stranger has of a company. In my experience of visiting and waiting around in hundreds of reception areas, I have found maybe five that were operated within the bounds of etiquette. Almost all of them have a flaw, or something to feel somewhat slighted by.

What are the qualifications of a good receptionist?

- A receptionist should have a smile. Even at a superelegant company that peddles snob appeal, the receptionist should offer something besides a poker face to a stranger at her gates.
- She should be cordial and polite. So many receptionists appear bored, and that is perhaps understandable. But it is not the fault of the visitors, and she should try not to take out her frustrations on them.
- A receptionist is not afraid to pronounce names correctly, and she should have some idea of who works in the company on her floor.
- She should tell the person she is chatting with about her boyfriend—or, if he *is* her boyfriend, ask *him*—to wait a moment while she finds out what you need. She is the only one who can get you through the locked door; she should always help you promptly.
- She should not look as if you've just asked her to strip down and perform the kootch when you ask her to check once again on someone who is a long time coming out to meet you.
- A receptionist should not eat lunch or anything else at the reception desk. It looks very bad to have people eating in any area where visitors are being received, yet I have seen this so often that it's appalling. Once I sat and watched a man with his tie hanging loose wolfing down a deli lunch at a desk while I and another visitor sat and waited. It was like watching a dog feed. Then he got up, straightened his tie, put on his jacket, and loped over to the elevators and left. Employees should eat somewhere out of sight. Estée Lauder reportedly once fired a receptionist for eating at her desk. *Brava*, Mrs. Lauder.
- Receptionists should not chew gum.

- Receptionists should not tell you how tired they are, how sick they feel, or whatever the trouble is that day.
- Some companies do not mind, but it looks very bad for a receptionist to entertain people at her desk. It is tough being a receptionist, and lonely on the front, but long visits and chats that are best conducted at lunch or in the women's room should not be held there.
- The receptionist should be able to converse in the native tongue of the country the office is located in, and she should have a passing familiarity with the foreign language that is most likely to be spoken periodically among visitors to that office. I have more than once called on or telephoned an American company and had to fight my way through a language barrier because the receptionist didn't speak English very well. Some strange sense of chic, one supposes, has made them right for the job, but it doesn't expedite business.

Qualifications

You must tell a receptionist how you want the phone answered. It must be done properly, not in an offhanded way, or with a harried rush to the voice, or in a bored manner. The company name should be spoken clearly, not just the phone number. People generally are aware which company they are calling (although not always), but few people remember a phone number immediately after dialing it. This is a psychological fact. You can save confusion by having your receptionist answer the phone by saying the company name, then good morning or good afternoon.

Too many receptionists do not know how to use a mouthpiece, placing their mouth either too close or somewhere out of range. Too many slur the company name so it is not audible to the caller. A receptionist should try to minimize phone time by doing things correctly and politely so as not to spark confusion or irritation in the caller.

A receptionist also should have the time to handle calls properly. If you receive too many calls, hire two receptionists or install private lines for all personnel.

A reception area should be clean, first of all, easy to identify as a reception area, and not hidden in some enclave where a stranger has difficulty finding it. The most exasperating thing that can happen to a visitor is to walk into an office that has no clearly defined reception desk, where there are people doing their work, and to be totally ignored by everyone, including the man who is sitting at the desk right by the door. It is good manners for the first person who is going to be seen by visitors to let them know where they are and ask if he or she can help. It happens more often than not that a visitor is ignored, or gets a mumbled something and a vague wave toward the general area behind the mumbler, then silence.

Bona fide reception areas should provide seating, perhaps something to read, and an ashtray. The receptionist should be able to offer coffee to visitors who must be delayed for an overlong time. Magazines are also a nice touch, but not necessary. Seating should be so designed that a man in a suit on a sweltering day will not sink so far back into the cushions that everything rides up and sticks beneath his arms.

The worst reception area I ever spent a half hour in was the size of a Super-Beetle and seated two. There were some art constructions on the walls placed exactly so that you banged your head on the wooden frames as you sat down, and they kept you in a position something akin to the way you would have had to sit in a medieval dunking stool. It looked great if you stood up, which I did for a half hour. The receptionist at one point said it was all right if I sat down, and I told her politely that I would stand. Later this same company moved to new larger offices, and that was where I got to see the man eat his lunch.

If someone manning a reception area is serving double duty as a secretary, he should try to keep his grousing and anger for times when visitors are not present. The same day I watched the man eat, I also had to listen to the receptionist get mad because he had to put a call through to someone who didn't pick up. He asked no one in particular why the stupid son of a bitch couldn't pick up his goddamned phone without his having to go the devil back to his office every time to tell him. My mind reeled with sarcastic replies, but I refrained from telling him.

Quiet on the Front

It is not a good idea to allow people to hang around the reception desk; they may get carried away and provide a noisy atmosphere, which is—or should be—undesirable. (If you run a record company, perhaps you will think it's all right, since sound is your bread and butter.) It is very difficult for a stranger to approach a noisy group of people under any circumstances. To have to face up to a group of people carrying on at a reception area is a real turn-off. The person would be within his rights to turn around and leave and call from outside. But then he'd still probably have to go through the switchboard at the reception area.

Besides observing the rules of etiquette, a reception area should be strictly organized to screen people carefully. Crime is a big problem in corporations, especially at lunchtimes, and your receptionist should be in a position to make sure that she knows exactly where each guest is going and what he or she looks like. If she is occupied with many other fun things, her efficiency is cut down.

7

THE BOSS
MYSTIQUE

MANY PEOPLE, UPON reaching positions of authority, feel they are no longer bound by the rules of etiquette. Rudeness is no more attractive in the personality of an executive—even a corporation head—than it is in a smart-alecky whiz kid. There are those who feel it is an interesting character trait to order people about as if they were cattle, and, like some Turkish sultan, to threaten all sorts of dire consequences if such orders aren't carried out to the letter. But such behavior is actually boring and obnoxious and makes the tyrants look like fools. Bad manners in a boss can actually be detrimental to his career, since people are less willing to cooperate with a nasty person and he will find his employees' productivity more and more difficult to maintain.

A boss must always bear in mind that he or she occupies a position of authority only to facilitate the function of business. It is not a license to threaten people with their jobs, to treat them as underlings, or to lord it over them. A boss is as much bound to say "Please" when giving a directive as anyone else. It is even more important for a boss to say "Thank you" when something is performed well, since the people working under him derive their incentive primarily from the boss.

Employees are under an obligation to cooperate with the boss to get a job done well, even brilliantly if the time calls for it. The boss is there to direct business, not to listen to personal problems (unless they affect work) and certainly not to do the job for the employee. In all boss-employee relationships the respect must be mutual; the employee must consider the boss's humanity just as much as the boss must consider those who work for him.

Good manners at the top—or anywhere near the top—reflect your sense of yourself as a successful person. They also are a display to others that you are secure enough in your position to be calm, to consider the needs of those who work for you, and to let them know that you can handle your position of power. If that statement seems a little extreme, remember that if you can't handle everyday politeness, if you are so easily tilted by job pressure that you can't apply simple amenities to your working relationships, then people may be fearful of what you will do in a serious emergency. What decision will you make? Will you crack under the strain? Whether the impression is true or not has little to do with it; your competence will be in doubt.

THE DANGLING AX

The worst kind of boss is the one who feels it necessary to constantly remind the people who work for him that he can fire them, or that their jobs or raises are secure only by his grace. This is not true, in the first place, or should not be. A good boss always knows that a person is in a job because he or she does it well. There are bosses who expect a certain amount of self-effacement from their staff people. Such types encourage this by favoring the people who are willing to grovel a little and cater to their egos. This is the worst kind of insult to professionals or co-workers. It is, in effect, saying that the way a person performs on the job isn't as important as the way he or she responds to the boss's jokes.

The bottom line of any boss-employee relationship at any level is that the boss can fire the employees under him. It is very bad manners to use that fact as a joke, and it is even worse manners to use it as a whip. I know of one woman who told her associate that she had read a psychological report that found that people were more afraid of losing their jobs than anything else. This woman then proceeded to use the words ". . . or I will fire you" every time she wanted to emphasize the importance of any project that had to be done well. The woman had a very difficult time keeping people, and eventually her joke backfired.

Do not use firing as a weapon. If someone should be dismissed, then do it. If you plan to keep him or her on and want improvements, then work with the person to obtain them. To constantly threaten termination is a despicable practice and indicates that you are not competent to find any practical solution to common workday problems.

UNREASONABLE BOSS

Some bosses tend to give assignments and directions to the employee either too quickly or in a way that is vague. Some go further and launch into angry tirades when questioned on the directions or asked to speak more slowly. No employe needs to take such abuse. The boss must be informed seriously and firmly that he is out of order. If the boss counters with the statement "If you don't like it you can leave," then say that leaving is not the issue but your rights as a human being are, and as long as you are there you will expect fair and decent treatment.

FEAR OF FIRING

Many people do not stand up to abusive bosses for fear of losing jobs or being transferred. Actually, another job, when possible, may be better; but one should not take abuse of any sort on the basis of keeping a job. Laws exist for the purpose of protecting employees from such treatment. If you are the victim of an abusive, unreasonable boss, look up your rights and go from there. It is possible that a company may be liable for a suit if an employee takes abuse as part of the requirement for not getting fired. This is why unions were started.

CRITIQUE THYSELF

People in very high executive positions should remember that they are imbued with a certain mystique that comes with financial success and administrative power. It is up to them to have the insight into themselves and others to know when their actions are appropriate. Most top executives are judged mainly by the way they behave, since not many people have a clear view of how they perform their jobs. The only traits of a top executive which are frequently discussed by most of the workers in the company are his or her temperament and whether he or she is "nice" or "not nice" to the people who come directly in contact with them.

This niceness cannot be rated too highly, and many people in lower or middle management positions tend to think it doesn't matter all that much. In fact, politeness in any position of authority is essential. I stood on a street corner in New York once and watched a foreman of the Transit Authority berating one of his workers, who was across the street, calling him a "stupid son of a bitch" at top voice in front of his co-workers and passersby.

I also watched the publisher of a sophisticated magazine do the same thing to his new secretary, using essentially the same invective, in front of almost as many people. Fortunately for the recipient of such a lambaste, the person doing the screaming is the one looked at in disgust. It never reflects badly on the person being attacked, even when the person is actually in the wrong. The use of flamboyant bad manners always immediately puts the user in the wrong and makes him look bad.

I was told a story of one vice-president of a data processing company who had become rather overwhelmed by his own success. Some people in the office decided to get together and buy him a silver cigarette lighter for his desk after he'd won an award, even though they disliked his general attitude. With mock modesty he told his secretary, "I don't want people buying me gifts like this— all I want is their respect and admiration."

The secretary looked at him straight in the eye and said, "If I were you, Mr. Franklin, I'd settle for the lighter."

A person who supervises other people must always remember that his actions no longer have a limited range. His moods, sarcastic remarks, and chance statements can be taken more seriously than they were when he was not in charge. He can affect the mood of the entire company. Because he has authority, he also has some power. I know of one executive who liked a casual, family-type atmosphere. His favorite "joke" was to suddenly say, when anyone disagreed with him about anything, "You're fired," then laugh. If he had looked, he would have seen that no one was chuckling with him.

Whatever one feels about his own position of power, one must realize that the authority is real and people are generally very much afraid of being fired. You can't joke about people's security or survival. Apart from the psychological motives, it is also extremely bad manners to rub people's noses in the fact that you have authority over them. This attitude indicates that you see them more as underlings than colleagues; that you think of them as servants instead of co-workers you need to get the job done. This causes them to become demoralized and resentful and to lose interest in working for you. They hope for your professional demise or look for other jobs where the desks don't come equipped with kneelers and pews.

It does not always hold that a bad-mannered boss is also a bad executive. In fact, many highly talented people treat employees very badly indeed. It is also true that a rude boss may still inspire a certain kind of loyalty among his or her people. In these cases the boss gives something else that is so valuable that it overrides the obnoxiousness of his personality and makes it worthwhile for his staff to support him. The boss may provide a fertile ground for his people to expand creatively, to try new things, to take chances that would not be possible anywhere else. Workers may complain about the boss's tiresome remarks and nagging ways, but they are still happy in positions that are beneficial to them.

It is not necesasry to treat people badly at all, of course, but there are some people who are emotionally or psychologically sick. They are not able to deal with being nice and accepting niceties; they have a need to treat people under them badly or underhandedly. Because they also are talented and there is nothing else in their personalities that make them unable to function, they reach positions of power. Some of them compensate in other ways, such as paying large salaries or providing creative freedom, to salve their guilt. Employees of such people must realize that there is little that can be done except to work around these compulsive, driven people and to accept whatever special benefits go with the discomforts.

One wonders how these people do get to high positions, but it happens. When young people start out in careers, these qualities are either dormant or not pronounced enough to be seen as illnesses. Self-made bitterness, disillusionments on other levels, the fact that success is never the fantasy we make it when we're young and starry-eyed—these things nourish the seeds of nastiness later on.

It is always refreshing to work for a highly successful boss who has gained wisdom and gentleness through the years, as well as power and money. Unfortunately, too many people spend all their energies clawing their way to the top and none of them in stepping back periodically to develop personally. Remember when dealing with any superior that success is a very difficult thing for anyone to handle.

LEADING BY EXAMPLE

Any company leader is in a position where he or she must set the standard for the kind of behavior expected of the employees and executives lower down in the company. This is what ultimately establishes the company's reputation and image. If a company has a reputation either as an unpleasant place to work or as a great place to work, it comes from the way everyone interacts with one another. And a good reputation and image are important for several reasons. They mean that the company will have an easier time attracting and keeping talented people. There is no doubt that people will prefer to stay with a company that has a comfortable atmosphere rather than accept a job for more money at a company where morale is low. I once knew a very talented person who gave up a new job that paid considerably more to return to his previous job for his original pay just because the atmosphere was so much more pleasant there.

A GOOD JOB, WELL DONE

Compliments, kind words, and a display—minimal though it may be—of the regard you have for your people will achieve more results than a demand for excellence. Compliments are important. People at all levels of business need them and respond to them—especially when they come from the top man or woman. But they must be genuine and used appropriately.

You can't go chattering, "You're doing splendidly, splendidly," as a stock remark to everyone. Nor can you keep a joviality going at all times. It's irritating to be complimented every time you blow your nose; but the well-deserved compliment for a job well done is something that everyone needs.

Although compliments on personal matters should be discreet or even nonexistent, praise for work is essential to any employee since it is the best gauge he or she has of his or her performance. Praise is a proven incentive when it comes from a boss, but it must be genuine and believable. A boss does not need to search for things to praise, but giving special notice to special achievements should become routine.

FLATTERY GETS YOU NOWHERE

Should you compliment your boss? This issue becomes somewhat tricky, since you run the risk of being called a sycophant or one of the less formal synonyms. Looking over some vintage "boss-lady" films from the forties, one would gain the distinct impression that the only way for a man to move up under a female employer is through flattery and romance. This is probably one of the worst approaches a man can take with a woman boss. It is also an insulting way for a woman to approach a male boss. Any kind of extolling of good looks, ability, or whatever should be avoided except under circumstances where your integrity cannot be called into question.

If a man walks into his female boss's office and says, "You really look wonderful today," she may be annoyed by the remark if she is engrossed in the day's business. If you are at a glittering gala and your female boss comes in wearing a Michaele Vollbracht original, your compliment would be viewed more as a mark of good taste than flattery.

It is generally not in good taste to compliment your boss—whatever sex either of you is—on physical appearance. If your boss has been ill, takes a sabbatical, and comes back looking great, then a comment is acceptable; it is less a compliment and more a verification that the vacation worked.

BOSS BABY

Many people who are in managerial positions find that anger or emotionalism helps them get what they want. At least they think it does. They use outbursts of anger, play on guilt, work to destroy people's self-images, and even cry real tears at times to achieve their ends. Such people usually are pushed out of their jobs before they get too high up. Like babies, they are stopped before they get into a position where they can hurt themselves, and others.

It is extremely rude and unfair to use any sort of emotional outburst to force your viewpoint in a business situation. If a boss must scream to get his or her way, then his or her competence to lead should be reviewed. Besides being plain bad manners and an indication of immaturity, emotionalism upsets the working atmosphere for everyone around, even those not directly affected by the outbursts. It lends a negative air to the office and leaves people tense and unable to function for a while.

If you have a boss who uses anger as a frequent, daily part of his or her repertoire, you have the choice of confronting him or her with the fact that this behavior makes it impossible for you to function ably, or of looking for a new job.

If you have been publicly reprimanded or yelled at by your boss, you should tell him in private that you don't like it and he may not treat you in that way. If he threatens you or does not take the complaint well, then take a wait-and-see attitude. It is not likely that a boss who has received this rebuke will have the lack of style to repeat his error.

People who are bad-tempered in the office are usually very much aware of it and are simply unwilling to exert themselves to use self-control. There is no reason for anyone to tolerate such behavior from a boss at any level. A complaint should be made directly to the person, or to someone who can handle it.

Remember this much about anger: If a person who has always been reasonable to work with undergoes a change in behavior and begins resorting to emotional outbursts, he or she should be made aware of it. Such a significant personality change is an indication that there is some physical or emotional—sometimes mental—problem. At times it may mean the person needs a break; I know of one case where it was caused by an undetected brain tumor. You should not let a sudden change in behavior go unremarked, since there is always a cause for it.

Successful top executives agree that the best demeanor to adopt in business is one of even-handed, even-tempered behavior. If anger is to be used, use it wisely and briefly and very infrequently. Business, they say, is a place to utilize business practices. There are no problems, only solutions. If you stay calm, you can find a solution more reliably than if you blow up.

Your colleagues look to you for predictable behavior. You cannot be erratic and expect also to be a rock and the pivot of the company. They must know what to expect from you even if the outcome is original or surprising.

MY FRIEND, THE BOSS

It is difficult for a boss to be friends with the people who work for him or her. At times it happens that one person in a department will be promoted and his friends now in essence work for him. Some people actively cultivate their staff socially under the impression that strong pesonal ties make it easier to count on company loyalty, or simply because they like the people they work with.

It is necessary for any boss to maintain a certain objectivity, if not distance, from the people he heads in business. It is not necessary to be aloof, although many high-level executives find that this is the best policy.

It is not bad manners to make a discreet separation between one's personal and business associates. Nothing is static in business. People ask for raises; good employees may go bad and need to be dismissed. An objective person can handle these matters more clearly and fairly if there is not the complication of an emotional tie involved in the decision.

If you are already friends with people you work with and are moved up, then the only way to handle your new position and keep your friends is to handle each situation as it occurs. Whenever any business problem arises concerning a friend, you can treat it objectively and make it plain by your actions that you cannot favor a person as a friend any more than his or her talent warrants.

Hiring Friends

There is always a temptation to hire people whom you know and with whom you already have a strong rapport. This natural impulse is often a good idea, but it can also easily backfire when the friend you always were delighted by, whose dinner-table viewpoints were so original and innovative, turns into a monster that you hired. I watched this happen once when an idealistic editor hired a friend to come on as creative director to revamp his magazine. The person had wonderful ideas and proceeded to put them all into operation. After we spent one deadline, then another, sitting around waiting for his writers to tell us where the assigned manuscripts were, then watched the advertisers recoil from the final product that finally came off the press, the editor had to save his own skin and everyone else's by firing the friend.

Criticizing Friends

The big problem that arises with hiring friends is that it is difficult to tell them they are wrong when the time comes. Everyone entering a new job is tacitly considered to be on trial for the first six months or so. At the end of that time you, the employer, must tell the friend that it's "go" or "no." Friends also have a tendency to think their jobs are being done more or less on a casual basis, that they aren't quite under the same strictures that govern run-of-the-mill employees. They may blurt out familiarities or sarcastic retorts and exhibit a general lack of respect for you as the boss. This can place you in an awkward position, make others on staff resentful, and lead to a general breakdown in discipline, morale, and productivity. All that just because you hired a friend.

If you approach a friend to come work with you, you will usually be viewed as asking a favor. If the friend is in need of a job, your offer can come across as charity. The etiquette when hiring a friend, under any circumstances, is to make it clear, over dinner, on the eve of the hiring, that the friend is expected to conduct himself or herself as an employee at the office. The fact that you have a special rapport can enhance the creative aspects of the job and get better results, but the base of the interaction must be business. If it comes time to fire the friend or for the friend to quit, it usually doesn't hurt the friendship. I know of no case, even on the *I Love Lucy* show, where friends broke up permanently over an aborted business partnership.

Don't let the rest of the staff know that the person is your close friend. It may cause instant resentment to flame up, especially if someone else on the staff felt he or she was in line for that particular position. The situation must be played down; your social life must be kept as separate from the office as before, until you institute a secondary business friendship as well. Remember, taking on a friend as an employee is the same as taking on one as a roommate: you may get along fine when there is distance, but you may not translate that smoothly into living together.

Maintain a certain business reserve; make sure the friend knows that certain parts of your friendship are off limits to discussions of business; and by no means make yourself totally available at home to hearings about business situations. Keep the two lives divided.

THE BABY-SITTERS

Many unmarried executives who are superbusy on the job often try to maintain some semblance of a personal life as well. One of these attempts may include having a pet cat or dog that needs watching when the executive must go out of town. It is always best not to rely on co-workers or secretaries or any business associates in the office to help in these situations. Friends, paid sitters, or kennels must be the avenues you will explore for animal sitters, house watchers, or whatever else may need surveillance when you're away.

I have always found it curious that many people who have expensive things in their homes will ask other people to live in while they're away. Unless the person being asked is out of an apartment or needs to get away from his or her own home, the etiquette is to avoid asking in the office for help of this kind.

Some people in the office do offer themselves as help, and though this seems like a terribly nice offer to make, it should be refused when possible. A secretary, for instance, who starts by ingratiating herself or himself in this personal way may be using it as a substitute for adequate performance in the office. It should also be remembered that many people lie in wait for these opportunities, doing a good job at first, gradually ingratiating themselves and interweaving themselves into the boss's personal life, until they reach a point where they are slacking on the job. Due to guilt, the boss cannot fire them, and he ends up with a cat-sitter when a secretary is vitally needed.

If you find yourself in this situation, steps must be taken to reimpose a professional relationship. Talk to the person, reestablish the ground rules, and if that doesn't work, find a new assistant. No one should be allowed to play on guilt to keep a job. It has been my experience that people who are available to watch the boss's affairs regularly are looking for homes, not careers or jobs. Even talented people may fall into this lazy lull, spending more time feathering a nest than pursuing creative advancement. People who are hard at work on the job have no reason to watch the boss's cat; they know their worth and they know what business is all about. To ask such people to take on the chores of your life is an insult to them; it assumes they have nothing better to do. People who are serious at their work will have no fear about refusing such a request. If it happens that you are already friends and the person's job is not dependent on your goodwill, and the person also offers help periodically, then that is a different matter. In general, however, it is best not to place yourself in a position of being indebted to any co-worker or employee.

PERSONAL PROBLEMS

In the experience of many bosses it happens that an employee will have to reveal his or her personal problems. This sharing must only be based on the fact that some personal troubles can affect one's performance on the job. An impending divorce is something that a boss may have to consider when viewing a valuable employee's current performance. As a boss it is necessary to realize that personal crises, from illness to deaths in the families to love affairs, must be viewed sympathetically. Nobody goes through life without some trauma, and any employee has the right to expect that his company will return his loyalty with understanding when he cannot perform up to par.

If the personal crisis makes it impossible to work at full capacity for longer than a reasonable length of time, then it is up to the employee or the boss to broach the subject and make some sort of change in the person's employment status. The length of time that should be allowed is usually dependent on the kind of work done by the employee and the needs of the company.

It is bad manners for any employee to expect the boss to listen to his or her problems as a sort of sob sister. The only reason to tell a boss your personal problems is to provide information that would explain your attitude or performance. It is good manners to give this information early on, rather than let the boss and co-workers suffer in ignorance. If the boss does suspect that a personal problem exists that is causing the employee to have a hard time at work, he or she should invite the person, privately, to share the knowledge. If the company has any sort of help available, it can be suggested. The boss, however, must never become a shoulder to cry on.

INABILITY TO COMMUNICATE

There are many people who are raised to positions of management based on their highly creative talent. When they reach these upper echelons they find themselves having to do less of the creative work that earned them their title and pay, and more administrative duties. They are very often not able to handle people well enough to direct them or to convey to them how they want a job done. Too many businesses insist on being blind to the fact that an ability to perform brilliantly does not necessarily include the ability to supervise the performance of others.

If you are afflicted with a boss who cannot tell you what he or she wants, you will have almost a surefire chance of being fired. The etiquette involved here is to take on the job yourself of showing the boss step by step what you need to know. You cannot really tell someone how to tell you how to do the job; but you should be very direct about your confusion and then ask specific questions on matters that are unclear.

Too many bosses who have this inability to communicate place the blame on the employee. You cannot hand anyone, especially someone new to the job, a piece of work and say, "Do it," even if the person has had similar experience in another job. This immediate, intuitive knowledge comes only after someone has been on the job long enough to learn it. In the meantime, it is the boss's responsibility to guide and direct.

WHEN BOSSES APOLOGIZE

Men or women at the top have to be more aware of their behavior for the simple reason that there is no one around to tell them to back off when they're going wrong. There are times when you may unfairly reproach someone in front of his peers. It is necessary to be aware of what you have done and to find a judicious way to make amends. Again that old fear of losing one's job has been touched, however unwittingly, or a person has been publicly humiliated and it's up to you to set things right again.

It is probably not a good idea to belabor an embarrassing situation by making a point of apologizing in public. This only focuses more attention on the mistake and may be interpreted as saying, yes, it was as serious as you feared. Follow up the faux pas with another remark that praises the wronged person, so he knows you didn't intend to put him down; or use the next convenient opportunity to take the person aside and indicate that you are sorry, and go on to some neutral or friendly subject. *Never belabor your gaffes.*

If you ever do lose your temper and actually chew someone out, then you are duty-bound to apologize either on the spot or in private. Then there is no requirement to belabor it by wearing ashes and sackcloth in public. Angry outbursts of that sort do occur, and wrong as they may be, they do not invalidate your whole career. To make a public apology about an embarrassing situation will only create another uncomfortable situation. Make your amends in private; then show yourself to be friendly toward the offended person at the next meeting.

If you have these outbursts frequently, you will not have to worry about saving your reputation, because there will not be a good one to save. A bad-tempered executive who makes a practice of humiliating or shouting at his people loses his clout and, rather than being perceived as someone to follow and imitate, is seen as a burden. You may delude yourself into thinking that people forgive these constant traumatic events, but they really hate them and look forward to a day when they won't have you to kick them around anymore.

TALKING BACK

It is not good etiquette to compound a boss's bad manners by retaliating with a remark in kind. The best approach for any person who has been insulted by someone of higher rank is to request a private meeting and state the dissatisfaction directly. If the person is very high up, it may be best to ignore it, since he may be vindictive and see you as insignificant enough to sacrifice to his own ego by getting you fired. Don't harbor grudges if you don't get an apology. If someone is bad-mannered enough to insult you without caring to make an apology, it is more a reflection on the insulter than on you.

I was told about a boss who had a bad habit of making puns and rude remarks out of nervousness whenever meeting new people in a business situation. An associate had brought many people in to meet the boss to consider doing business with him, and the boss had always managed to insult each one in some minor way. Since this was done out of pure tension, there did not seem to be a solution. The associate eventually had to discuss the matter, since part of the business was meeting new people. He pointed out the boss's problem and asked to be allowed to conduct the meetings himself. It worked well. The boss was freed of the source of tension, and the associate was able to convey decisions to uninsulted prospects later on.

There seems to be little reason for some of the common problems one encounters among executives these days, since there are so many avenues of executive improvement available, in the way of encounter groups or private sessions. If you sincerely believe you, or your boss, can benefit from such programs, you should discuss the possibility of using them.

RUDENESS AT THE TOP

Many years ago I had to interview a famous executive who headed a large corporation. The man was reputed to be difficult, but his public image was one of magic and success. Several other top executives of the company were at the meeting as well. During the interview, one executive leaned forward and said to the great man, "Charles, wouldn't it be a good idea if we could provide pictures to go with the story?"

The famous man turned, twisted his face into a look of mocking pity, and said, "Well, if you can figure some way to get pictures of something that hasn't been produced yet, you're smarter than I am." The implication was that no one was smarter than he was, and he smirkingly scanned his other executives like a teenage gang leader looking for backup. The room was momentarily silent, and I could feel the tension that they worked under daily.

Several years later, by chance, I had to do another story on the same man, this one a personal interview on his style and personality. He kept us waiting, photographers, stylists—even his own people—for four hours, well into the evening. Finally he walked in, went up to his executive, and said to him as if he would never catch on, "You see, Jim? We can't be bothered with things like this."

During the rest of the session he basked in his ego, asked for the pictures to be retouched, and was charm itself. It was clear that his ego had been fed well by making us wait all afternoon, then taking the time to embarrass his executive in front of us all.

There was no way to deal with him except politely to tolerate his behavior, since he would have walked out on us otherwise. When dealing with anyone in a position of tremendous power, it is totally up to them to maintain good manners, since there is no one who can take them to task for it. The only rule of etiquette that people in high positions should remember is the statement by Malcolm S.

Forbes: "People who matter are always aware that everyone else matters, too."

CRITICISM

There are times when criticism is necessary, but the manner in which it is presented must be discreet. One should never attack an associate's intelligence or ability when making a judgment on his or her work. If a mistake has been made, it should be treated as human error and something that requires a solution or an adjustment. If the person has done something that is a result of laziness or stupidity, it is best to remember that the person is embarrassed enough by the fact that it has happened and everyone knows about it.

Any reprimand should be made in professional terms, not presented as an attack. If the incompetence continues, then you have the avenue of dismissal to use. No boss-associate relationship should ever dissolve into personal scolding.

THE SMALL STUFF

Executives of high level should not concern themselves unduly with matters that are clearly the province of managers lower down in the company echelon. It may be a character quirk for a top exec to go through the offices on his way home and turn out the lights in the empty areas. It is also a matter of choice if a president of a company wants to go through the secretary's wastebasket to see if she throws away paper clips. (Yes, we know of one top woman executive who does that.)

Many years ago I knew of a company president who made an issue about the fact that one of the employees was burning incense in her office. Since the windowless office had bad circulation, the young woman felt it would freshen up her environment. It was vetoed after several days of flurry and memos handed down. It turned out that the president equated incense with smoking pot and was convinced that it was illegal, too. The woman decided to end the hassle and use fresh flowers instead.

To avoid making fools of themselves, high-level executives should quietly glean some facts about a situation before making dicta. Employees have their prerogatives to make their lives comfortable. If you don't provide windows, don't prohibit incense . . . or at least find out what incense is first.

TAKE MY WIFE—AND FAMILY

If you have a husband or a wife, you must be careful when bringing him or her into the areas connected with work. The mere presence of the boss's spouse in a business situation runs the risk of causing tension. People never know what may or may not insult the spouse (or the son or daughter) of their boss. If the spouse is left alone, someone has to take the lead. The spouse probably has little idea what to discuss with people who work with his or her mate; the employees feel they must converse and are afraid to touch on any subject for fear of stepping on toes.

Do you compliment the wife's dress, or do you ignore her appearance altogether? Do you ask about the children, or does one of them have a drug problem? The situation seems fraught with dangers. The spouse generally must be careful not to step on toes, too.

Some executives keep their mates strictly separate from the business; others interweave their business and daily life so tightly that there is no such thing as a friend out of the businesss. That's always risky unless the wife is really tuned in to the whole business and likes it well enough to hold her own.

Remarks between employees and boss's family members should be kept cheerful, polite, and perfunctory. If the spouse happens to be well integrated with the corporate "family," then conversation is much easier, since everyone is familiar enough with the spouse to speak naturally.

It is polite to offer to fetch drinks or hors d'oeuvres for the boss's wife or husband, but not to fuss and be solicitous. He or she should be treated as any other new business associate you might meet at a similar function.

If an employee does try to gain favor with the boss via the spouse, the spouse should provide a smiling formality and keep the conversation superficial. Any answers to questions or probes about the boss's feelings on business should be fended off with some remark about keeping Church separate from State.

Entertainments, sports, schooling, and personal background are all agreeable topics for conversation. The spouse should never make comments about the state of the company's health unless he or she is willing to become entangled in a tricky conversation that may lead to tension or gaffes on everyone's part.

JUNIOR

The time comes in most top executives' lives when they have to deal with whether or not their offspring will come into the business, and if so, whether the kids will be talented enough to take over the top spot. This is not a serious consideration unless you actually own the company, but even if you don't, your son or daughter may want to follow in your footsteps. The situation is, of course, no problem at all if you are not in an ownership position; fellow workers or executives welcome the children of a longtime respected colleague and make things easy for them.

The sons or daughters of an owner, however, are very often damned if they do and damned if they don't. They usually can't be as free to make jokes or remarks or interact on the same level as other young execs just starting out. They are seen as having the ear of the top man, and people make an adjustment every time they want to tell a joke, express a gripe, or goof off for an hour. It's not the kids' fault; it's just the way it is.

Parental Duty

Tell your executives what the situation is; instruct them to train and help, but not favor, the scion. Make yourself open to the possibility that the kid just might not have what it takes and may have to be flunked out. Leave him on his own for enough time to prove or disprove himself, just as you would another employee. Then, if he exhibits a special talent for the business, you will be correct in moving him up at a rate that is acceptable to all concerned. Make sure that all other people in the company are aware of what your plans are for the legacy, but also make sure you never kill off someone else's career to favor your child.

Until the son or daughter does get to the point of having a history in the company and people are used to him or her as a familiar member of the company, things may be awkward. But this passes once the "heir" has put in a few years and no one thinks of her or him as the boss's kid anymore. It then truly becomes a family business.

Once you have retired and still visit the company—even maintaining an office there—make it clear that the decision making is passed from your hands, and that your ear is mainly for hearing requests for advice from the new top person rather than giving opinions off the cuff. It takes a great man or woman to gracefully give up in a real way, and when the new replacement is your own offspring, it calls for a great deal of tact, discretion, and etiquette.

Hanging In There

The young heir apparent is under a special obligation to show the people who will be working for him that he is worthy of the position he will take. The traditional role of the boss's "kid" is to overkill trying to prove his worth. It is not in fact a bad idea. If one is going to take over and run a business, one owes it to oneself to make sure one is the best qualified. The side benefit of gaining everyone's loyalty and admiration is part of the job.

8

A CALL
IS WAITING

THESE DAYS THE telephone is synonymous with business. Most business dealings are conducted by phone, especially since the mails are such a mess and since we often must deal daily with people who live thousands of miles away from us. Entire business relationships and friendships are based solely on the sound of a voice. You can spend years doing business with someone on the phone and never see his or her face. You may even know all about his or her personal life, share deaths in the family and romantic involvements, and help each other in many ways, and never meet face to face.

On the negative side, the telephone lets rude people get away with a lot, simply because you are only able to be in touch as long as the phone call lasts and there is no way to get back at someone or to prove that you've been maligned during a phone call. A receptionist at her desk, face to face, may be very polite to you, since you are there in the flesh. Two days before, she may have put you on hold forever when you called and been flip about it as well.

The telephone is a fun instrument. It is also a wonderful power tool, since you can be very political without giving away secrets through facial expressions, sweaty palms, or nervous mannerisms. People can be very confident over the phone since they are only presenting a part of themselves for judgment, and it is easier to focus on making your voice work than pulling together a whole facade of sight, sound, smell, and touch. I have carried on whole interviews with important people from home, stark naked, and they never knew it. The phone is wonderful.

HELLO? HELLO?

One of the worst things that can be done on the telephone—among so many bad things that are done—is to let the thing ring more than three times before it is picked up. A person who calls a company during normal business hours should be able to get a pickup quickly. The worst offender I have ever encountered was a nonprofit organization in New York, where a friend works. I have come to know that I must let the phone ring for as many as thirty times if I want it picked up. The shortest time I have ever waited was eight rings.

In discussing the matter with my friend, I discovered that the office manager was slovenly and was to be replaced. Until then they had to live with missed calls, no-show lunch dates, and the other flack from people who couldn't get an answer. It seemed to me that the receptionist would have had the common sense to answer the phone, but she didn't. She wasn't trained correctly. If she was on one call, she did not place it on hold and pick up the incoming call. Or if she was chatting with friends down the hall, the phone was left to ring until the day she decided to mosey over and answer it.

A more common exasperation is to have the phone picked up immediately and get this:

"Acme Promotional Company—will you hold pl—[Click]."

This is very irritating, because you may be calling from a pay phone or calling long distance. Needless to say, Ma Bell, with her usual antagonism, won't let you wait more than thirty seconds on hold if it's person to person, so you end up with a noose around your neck hoping for the sheriff to arrive.

Often you are left holding for a long time, and sometimes, before you can ask for your party, the receptionist has you back on hold again to take another call. It appears that she is interested only in answering the phone, not in putting people through. It's almost as if she is collecting people to see how many can be put on hold at one time.

Any company that must handle a great many calls should install a system that can process them—or should hire a person who has some skill in answering.

The problem becomes even more acute when you must leave a message and the receptionist cannot take your name correctly. In such a case it is best to hang up and try later or very early the next morning, or to write or send a telegram. It is not rude to mention the poor answering service when you finally do reach your party, but it probably won't do much good. If you do not expect to have to call again, don't bother. If you must have future contacts, ask the person to call you and tell him why.

Incoming calls at a business office should be answered within two or three rings and the call put through within thirty seconds, or enough time should be given to take a proper message.

WHISTLE WHILE YOU WAIT

Some companies play music for you over the phone while you are kept on hold. This presumably is to make it less irritating to be kept waiting for a long period. Personally, I hate it; if I am making business calls, I try to use the hold time to review what I want to say to the person I'm calling, and a burst of molasses music scrambles my thoughts. By the time the person picks up, I'm ready to snap at him.

Music on the hold button also indicates a certain casualness that is not appropriate to business: it is in effect saying that, yes, you will be kept on hold for a long time, and it is done often enough to make it worth playing music to soothe you, you impatient beast. Worse, it means the company accepts the policy of keeping people waiting for long periods of time.

ON PERMANENT HOLD

One of the biggest irritations in business is being put on hold and forgotten. This happens sometimes by accident, sometimes through carelessness on the part of the receptionist. Sometimes it happens through incompetence. I used to call a friend at a cultural organization periodically. As an atmosphere device they used a person from the country whose culture was nourished through the foundation, and she could not handle the phones very well if more than one call was coming in. She would become extremely flustered, try to organize her thoughts, and tell you the most intimate details of what Mr. Smith was doing at the moment and why he couldn't come to the phone just yet.

It was impossible for her to put you through in these cases, yet she didn't want you to hang up. The matter was usually settled by your being put on hold. And forgotten. The only way to handle such matters is to call back, tell the receptionist she left you on hold, and ask to be put through or leave a message.

IDENTIFY BY NAME

When answering a phone, the receptionist should identify the company name. As mentioned earlier, it is often the custom to identify by the phone number, especially if an answering service picks up, but this can be confusing since most people think in terms of names, not numbers. There is no proper response to such a greeting and it should not be done.

When answering your own private line, it is best to identify yourself by name; when picking up a general line in a certain department, identify the department.

COVERING YOUR LINE

If you have a computerized phone system with different numbers for each individual, you may have a problem making sure your phone is covered. The best policy is to have the calls answered by the receptionist in your absence; it is not a personal favor, since it is assumed that your phone is being used for business. If you are away for a brief period, several people should arrange to answer one another's lines when possible, or the receptionist should be cued to pick up any phone that rings more than three times.

FIRST-TIME LOSERS

When you call a place for the first time, you are at several disadvantages. Some secretaries act as if you have a lot of nerve calling when you have never called before. The assumption seems to be that the boss does business only with old friends. This is clearly rude on the part of the secretary. Any new person who calls on legitimate business should have the opportunity to be presented to the correct person in the company.

It is not a good policy to call anyone out of the blue for a telephone conversation even for legitimate business. It is always better to send a letter first, telling the person what you want, then adding to the letter a paragraph saying: "I will, if it is convenient, call you within a few days to ask if we can set up an interview or discuss this subject further on the telephone."

This provides the addressee with some background, gives you an introduction so he knows your name, and gives him the opportunity to write back if he is not interested and does not want to hear from you. It also provides an opportunity for him to call you if he is interested. I have found that I always receive a polite response when I write before calling, and that the person—and sometimes the secretary—remembers my name so that the ice is broken, whether or not my services prove useful.

People have a natural hostility to a new person who calls on the phone; I believe it is a primary instinctual response rather than rudeness. When people know you ahead of time, even if you've only introduced yourself by letter, they will subconsciously be more receptive.

PERSONAL REFERENCES

It is all right to call a person in business without writing beforehand if someone else has already referred you. In this case, it would be absurd to write a letter in advance, since you have already been introduced. I find that even if the person does not remember the introduction, he or she will still be receptive to you. When researching this book I called someone and said, "Mr. Porter suggested I call you to interview you for my book." The response was warm and an interview was set up at a special hour for me.

When I arrived I again referred to Mr. Porter and was somewhat surprised when the interviewee did not know or remember who he was. It made no difference since, as he said, he receives so many calls that he cannot always put a face to a name. But we had a good inteview, despite the lapse of memory.

GETTING THROUGH

One public-relations executive in New York tells us that on a first introductory call, or when you are trying to find who the proper person is to talk to about your subject, "give as much information as possible, no matter how trying it is. Even if you must repeat the whole speech over and over to different people, maintain your patience and do so."

There are times when it is necessary to call a company to find out whom to talk to—to obtain a name. In this case it is best to remember that the receptionists and secretaries to whom you are routed and rerouted are trying to help and doing you a favor. To avoid being accidentally cut off, stay polite, no matter how trying it all becomes. There are times when there is no one to talk to; in that case, write to the president of the firm and ask for information on how to make contact with the right person.

It is always a good idea when calling or writing to anyone to use the name of another person in the company, even if you may not know that person. This gives you some clout and will help you stand out from the crowd of callers who don't know what they want or what they are doing.

Always remember when calling any company or person for the first time that the receptionists or secretaries have more to do than just handle your call. No matter what you want or who you are, be someone who requests, not someone who demands.

RETURNING CALLS

Every call should be returned at the earliest possible convenience. There are many executives who will not return calls they do not want to handle, as a way of discouraging the person from calling. This is very rude. If you do not wish to deal with a person on the phone, have your secretary give that information in a polite message directly from you. It is not impolite to handle certain callers in this way. A person does not have a right to speak directly to someone just because he calls. In this case business efficiency comes first. A secretary may always impart a message from her boss to a caller without being considered rude. In any case, all calls should be returned within one working day, even if the secretary calls to tell the caller the boss will return the call the following day. You never know when it's something *really* important.

Some important clients may not see it that way, and in cases where personal attention is required, the executive should be able to make that decision, or his secretary should be able to gauge whether the mood requires a direct voice-to-voice contact. In general, all callers should respect an executive's prerogative to have messages passed on through his secretary.

Persistent or unwanted callers who have proved themselves not to be useful to your business should be informed that you can see no further possibility of working together and that if you change your expectations, you will get back to them. If they continue to call and you do not wish to talk to them, you may either refuse to speak to them or tell them you are busy and will get back to them—then do not.

It is extremely bad manners to frustrate a caller who is unknown to you but is trying to reach you. A certain amount of time can be made available to hear the person's business, or, if you work through your secretary through necessity, to have her screen the caller and pass a message back that you are unable to accommodate him.

WHO DIALS/WHO ANSWERS

It is expected that a secretary will answer the phone for her boss. Sometimes the boss will answer it instead. Some people must have their secretaries make calls for them, and this is where trouble starts.

When you are busy, it is not rude to have a secretary make a call, then say, "This is Mr. Wilson's secretary calling for him to speak to Mr. Johnson. Is he in?" If Mr. Johnson is in, then Mr. Wilson should be on the line when he picks up. It is rude to make a call and say immediately, "Hold for Mr. Wilson, please," and expect the called person to wait. This assumes that Mr. Wilson's schedule is very busy and no one else's is. It is perfectly all right for a secretary of a busy person to make his calls; it is not all right to keep the party waiting once he or she is reached.

At times this is unavoidable—for example, when a person answers the phone himself instead of having a secretary pick up. In this case it would be rude for the called person to hang up before the caller gets on the line. One assumes that only superbusy people do not dial their own calls.

If one is cut off accidentally in the transaction, the policy is for the called party to wait until the caller's secretary calls back to avoid confusion and busy signals.

THE UNKNOWN CALLER

Many times executives forget names that they have heard before, or a message is left by an unknown caller. This is reason for your secretary to request some additional information, asking what the person is calling "in reference to." Some people dislike having to state their business to a secretary, but it is only good manners to do so. Another approach for the secretary or assistant—more polite than just "What is this in reference to?"—is "Will Mr. Jones know what this is in reference to?" If you are known to the person you are calling, you can say that it is a personal call or that you do business regularly with him or her.

If a name or phone number constitutes the whole message you receive and you don't know what the person wants from you, it is permissible to just call and say, "I am returning your call." The ensuing conversation will certainly inform you, spark your memory, or provide an opening to ask if you have been in touch before. It is permitted to ask to be reminded if you think you have talked to the person before but have forgotten. Business expediency takes precedence here.

PLEASE BELIEVE ME

It is possible that someone is lying when he or she tells you the person you want is in a meeting or not in when you call. This is still not a valid reason to call the person a liar or persist in a pushy way to question the person taking the call. Never say to a secretary: "Well, when is he going to be in? I've been trying to reach him for days!"

It's best to couch your impatience in terms such as "I'm sorry to be persistent. Can you tell me when the best time would be to call? It's important I talk to him by tomorrow."

This approach usually breaks down the wall of silence and you get something besides the formula. The secretary, who is human, responds and realizes she can get you off her case if she gives you some valid information.

THANKS ANYWAY

Most people today do not commonly use the words "Thank you" for many things that traditionally would require it. If you receive directions on the phone, a thank-you is in order. Some people do not expect it and hang up before you can say it; these people are not rude, but consider helping people communicate with the company to be part of their jobs.

The best thanks is to remain polite when it takes a while for someone to get you to the person you need on the phone. Spoken thanks are always appreciated, and an expression of gratitude for a special favor from a phone handler should be made.

VOICE MANNERISMS

Many people must be careful of how they use their voices. On the phone a friendly, gentle person may come off as being gruff, rude, or angry if the voice is not emanating from an aware person. If you must use the phone often in business and you are unsure of how it will come off, ask people to listen in or to judge your phone voice in a test call. Tiredness can make one sound unpleasant unless care is taken to "lift" the voice tone.

Speaking while in a semireclining position, as in an executive's chair, may change the voice quality. A woman who is rushed may unwittingly sound strident over the phone. Speaking too close to the mouthpiece or over its top may come off as unpleasant, casual, or careless to the person at the other end.

Be careful not to pull the phone away from your mouth as you are saying good-bye. It will sound to the person at the other end as if you can't wait to hang up. It's best to depress the button with your finger first, then replace the phone in the cradle if you can, especially if you are going to start talking to someone in the office.

It is as necessary to cough or clear your throat away from the receiver as it is to cover your mouth in a similar situation when talking face to face with someone. Always remember that on the phone you are talking into someone's ear. Act accordingly.

LEAVING MESSAGES

The easiest names in the world are often anathema to people. I once had a roommate named Ashbridge, and he never received a nonpersonal piece of mail with his name spelled right. It is always best to spell your name when leaving a message. I don't guarantee that it will always work: I spent three weeks doing a story with a company once, spelled my name for everyone I talked to, and arrived to be greeted all the way as "Mr. McVey."

It is important good manners to get a caller's name spelled correctly and to ask for the correct pronunciation when in doubt. A person's name is the representative of his ego. To get it wrong is almost an insult if there was adequate possibility of having heard it correctly said.

When you do call, it is utmost bad manners not to identify yourself when the person is unavailable. Do not say "Never mind" and hang up. This can be infuriating to the person taking the call. If you called, it is presumably important enough to leave some sort of message, even if it's only your name and the information that there is no message.

It's also polite to leave your phone number, even when you know the person has it. Most people prefer to read the number on a phone message rather than go to the extra trouble of having to look through a Rolodex. Even people who have wonderful memories for phone numbers may draw a blank when they are having a crazy day or returning ten different calls in a row.

Remember always when you call that you are using a person's time at work and if you do not leave a proper message, you may be inconveniencing that person during a busy day. Try to cooperate with the message taker, who presumably knows best how the boss likes to receive his or her messages.

When you make a call, always give your full name to the person who answers, unless you are calling a friend and the friend, not someone else, answers. To say "This is Bob, is Frank in?" may confuse the message taker, who knows of three different Bobs. The best reply to such a question is: "I'm sorry, I don't recognize your voice. What is your last name?"

MESSAGE MACHINES

It is rude to hang up on message machines, even though some people feel an unreasonable animosity toward these helpful robots. There is nothing more boring than listening to thirty seconds of dial tone when one is playing back messages. If your call is not important, still have the courtesy to leave your name and say the call isn't important. Always leave your number and the day you called, and say whether or not it is important to get back to you in a certain length of time. It is important when leaving a message to say which company you are from as well.

It is also rude to give an answering service a hard time when calling anyone. People who work for answering services are hired to pick up for a company and are geared only to pass on messages, not to handle secretarial chores or divulge company information. Remember that these services handle many different clients and are not privy to information about any of them. Leave your message and don't ask unreasonable questions.

PRIVATE LINES

With the advent of computer phones one may run into some irritating problems. So many companies these days install private lines throughout the company, with a separate number for each desk. Since these lines usually do not transfer a call to another number if one line is busy, you can run into a passel of dialings trying to locate someone near the office of the one you want. There is no way around this except to have the main number of the company and ask to be connected to that person's department.

If you have such a phone system, try to transfer people to correct extensions when possible, since they will have to dial again and it will cost them to make each call separately.

THE AVOIDANCE GAME

A very good secretary told me that the first requisite for her job was "How well can you lie on the phone?" The boss she works for needs defense against the barrage of phone calls that come into the office, since she is in a position to dispense a lot of work to various sorts of creative people, from photographers to artists to models to suppliers. Yet it is to her advantage to try to see everyone who calls because new talent and creations are her stock-in-trade. She must stay up to the minute, and besides, she likes to get to know unknowns who may be special.

"Some people are so incredibly persistent," the secretary said. "They will call ten times a day, after you already told them she'll get back to them as soon as she can. They don't understand she has priorities and a job to do of her own."

The necessity here is to be firm with overcallers. It is rude to call more than once on the same day if you have been told that the person you want will get back to you, unless there is an emergency. Then you should say that there is. It is all right to try again later the next day, but always give the person the leeway to get back to you when it is possible.

I had an editor who always returned calls, no matter how late she did it. She was superbusy, and I knew she would always call the next day or late on the day I called. She set aside certain hours to return her calls. If I kept calling until I found her free, she would have a stack of messages that she might think came after I talked to her, and she'd be wasting her valuable time keeping up with my pushiness.

If you are in a hurry, ask the secretary if she can give you some idea when the call might be returned, or explain why you need to talk to the person soon. And be damn sure you do have a need that will indeed be perceived as urgent, or you may lose out altogether.

You will probably not get what you want through telephone rudeness. This is the easiest kind of affront to handle: the person can give your message with the accompanying information that you acted like an SOB on the phone; or the message can be lost; or the boss may resent your attitude so much that you will never hear from him. The friend I mentioned above received a call from an agent who had been trying to get in touch with her; he started reading her out for taking so long to get back to him. She let him go on, then told him that she couldn't work with anyone who had his attitude, and eliminated him from her list.

Never express displeasure about having to wait for a phone call to get through. It is always best to accept the fact that you have gotten through at last and take that as the starting point for a positive business relationship. If you show friendly patience, the person will probably feel some obligation to give you special consideration and will feel more inclined to work with you.

WHEN TO BE RUDE

There are times when it is necessary to tell someone, in professional terms, to bug off. An editor once received a nasty phone call from a representative for an electric-shaver manufacturer complaining that his client wasn't mentioned in a story. The woman listened to him carry on about how his client was the largest manufacturer of that product and how any story leaving them out was not valid and on and on. She began trying to interject, but he was determined to lambaste her. No doubt his client was in the office and he was showing how effective he could be. Finally she had had enough of his verbal abuse and said quietly, "I will hang up on you if you don't calm down and talk to me in a civil manner."

There was a stunned silence; then he said, "I think you're very rude." But he did give her space and time to present her side of the case.

There is never any reason for anyone to accept abuse on the

phone or anywhere else in the name of business. Exasperation that engenders some temper tantrums is at times acceptable, but there is no reason to stay on the phone listening to someone vent his spleen. There are any number of good psychiatrists who will listen to paranoid ravings, and your business day need not be ruined doing it.

If someone uses profanity, it is acceptable to hang up, although it is only polite if you first ask them to refrain. It is not legal to use profanity on the phone, and this is another instance where nobody is being paid enough to take that kind of abuse.

If someone calls and asks the names and titles of employees without stating why he wants them, refer the person to the personnel department or tell him you don't give out that sort of information, say good-bye, and hang up.

If someone refuses to give his name and ignores requests for it, but persists in asking questions, don't answer any of them. If he persists in ignoring your request, hang up. Anyone who refuses to identify himself is eliminated from the category of business caller and need not be treated as anything but a crank caller.

WHEN TO HELP

Some sincere callers often need help in finding someone to give them information. If such people call and ask for "the publicity department," try to ascertain what information they want and pass them on to someone who might conceivably guide them. It may take time, since some people become shy when they think they are being a bother, but it may be worthwhile to help them. This is a common courtesy that most companies try to provide.

INTERRUPTIONS

One of the most common problems that occur is having the phone ring while you are in a meeting with someone in your office. Perhaps it's your lawyer calling on a Friday afternoon with important news he must tell you before he leaves for Tahiti on the 5:30 shuttle, or it may be your boss calling. You grin embarrassedly from behind the receiver; meanwhile, your guest is trying hard not to hear your conversation and is closely scrutinizing the picture of your dog on the wall.

The best way to handle an important call in this situation is to excuse yourself and take it in another office. It is very awkward to try to carry on an important call in front of a stranger who is positioned directly facing you and whose own meeting has been interrupted.

If the visitor works with you and can take a break to get coffee, it is polite to ask for privacy; but if you are with a group of co-workers, you must treat them as if they are outside guests and go to another phone.

It is best not to have phone calls coming into your line when you are having a meeting. Your guest deserves your best-quality attention, and the fact of his or her presence should preempt most phone calls.

The fact is that not all calls can be screened during a meeting, and in that case you can have the receptionist take them or, if you have a modular phone, disconnect the line so it won't ring in your office during the meeting.

One friend told me that he sat in an office during a meeting while his host got into a fifteen-minute harangue with his Spanish-speaking cook—using two languages and arguing in loud tones. If you take a call during a meeting, the burden of etiquette is on you. The caller does not know there is someone in the office with you. It is always best to tell him as soon into the conversation as you can. If the message is brief, take it and hang up quickly. If not, ask him to call back much later.

Do *not* tell the phone caller to call back in fifteen minutes or so. This is communicating to the office guest that he is being ejected soon. No matter how quickly the meeting may actually end, it is a jolt to hear a time limit stated to someone else. Tell the caller you will get back to him as soon as you can.

On the other end of the line, it is important never to keep the person on the phone when he says he can't talk. Don't try to squeeze in a question before hanging up. It makes the person look bad to his guest or exasperates him.

I knew one man who used to call a friend at his office and make deprecating remarks to the secretary who answered the phone. If the secretary said he was at the law library researching a case, the friend would say, "Oh, I'm *sure* he is . . . he's probably researching at the movies."

This is astoundingly rude and stupid, of course; even in jest this type of remark should never be made. If you are calling a friend at work, you must be especially polite and self-effacing to anyone else who answers the phone. The possibility of office gossip, as well as the need to protect a friend's business image, makes this imperative. Personal calls at work must always be considered in advance as possible unwanted intrusions.

PERSONALS

Whenever you do take personal calls at the office, it is good manners as well as good sense to be sure your conversation is not picked up by the ears of your secretary or co-workers. It is bad manners to subject people to chatter about your personal life. I had one editor who shared an office with me, and I spent most of my day listening to her call her network of friends. As she had fights with her lover, she would call various friends to get their opinions, to have them call the lover, to get back to her about what the lover said. . . . It was draining to try to concentrate on a manuscript about traveling through the Rockies in a trailer while she conducted weekly crises about everything from the Christmas goose to what went on at the poker party the night before.

FOOD AND DRINK

It is not polite to eat or drink when talking to people on the phone. Nothing can be more irritating than a close-up audio of someone's chicken sandwich. If you smoke, it may also be irritating to have your pipe clunking against the phone. I was told of one man who actually would excuse himself from a phone call to go get a cup of coffee, leaving the caller waiting on the line. Besides tying someone up during the business day, this kind of casualness is an affront to your caller.

ADVANCE PREP

Whenever you call someone to ask for some information, it is best to prepare yourself first. It is extremely irritating to receive a call from someone who needs information and who doesn't know exactly what that information might be, or someone who takes forever to ask a question. A stumbling, confused request is enough to obtain a stern reply from the person being bothered. Always write down exactly what you need to know in advance and have the queries in front of you. Write down the answers and information as it comes. Ask your questions as quickly and succinctly as possible.

Always have a pencil and pad poised to take information as you ask for it. If you call for a phone number, don't interrupt the person who is giving it to you by saying, "Wait, I need to get a pencil and paper." It makes you appear unprofessional.

ARE YOU READY?

Always ask a person first if you have called at a convenient time before launching into your spiel. It is a courtesy, even if the person is a friend. You must always assume that the person's time is valuable and give him the opportunity to return the phone call at a more convenient time. It may be that the person is not prepared to talk to you when you call, and it is courteous to provide some leeway.

It is always polite when someone calls you to assume that he is calling for a valid reason, even if you are superbusy. It is very rude to follow the example of a prima donna newspaperman who once said to a caller, "All you public-relations people have to do with your time is drive me crazy!"

There are certain aspects of making a business work that involve calling people—and certain people are in a position that they must expect a lot of calls. It is not polite to treat someone's profession as a bothersome and unimportant thing. If you can't handle a lot of calls coming in, then have someone screen them for you.

On the other hand, it is necessary to remember that your professional methods may be hard for some people to handle. It is necessary in business at times to take no for an answer. It is necessary at times to be rerouted to an appropriate party, no matter how much you feel the one you are talking to is the one you need. Trust the person to know best what information he or she can use and accept a referral or a detour or a refusal as part of the overall business picture. Don't argue with someone who says, "This is wrong for me."

There are times when the tension of the workday makes you impatient or short with people. If you find yourself being curt on the phone, do not be afraid to stop, back off, and say, "Excuse me if I sound impatient. I'm not meaning to be, it's been a trying day." Then be more civil for the rest of the call. Some people will offer to call back at a more convenient time, and if you feel you can handle the call more efficiently then, you may accept the postponement.

AVOIDING HOME CALLS

I once had a publicity person call me after we had met at a business lunch to thank me for the opportunity to get to know me, et cetera, and to express a few other niceties, at the end of which she smoothly said, in a polite, unexpected way, "And may I have your home phone number?" I automatically gave it to her before I could think of a reason not to. She had set up such an aura of etiquette it would have sounded rudely august to say, "I never give out my home phone to business acquaintances." As time went by, she became a close friend socially as well as an excellent business associate, so the matter was put down to good karma. If you do not want your home phone made public, you can say that it is more convenient to reach you at work and leave it at that.

If people do not respect the home phone as personal, the best course of action is to have someone you live with say, "I'm sorry, he isn't available. Please contact him at the office in the morning." There is no reason to feel it necessary to get back to the person unless you want to make the firm point that you do not take calls at home from business people. If you answer at home, you can make it clear on the spot.

The best way to discourage home phone calls is to refuse to give out your home phone number. If someone gets it from the phone book, you can politely say that the call is looked on as an imposition and that you will be available to talk during the workday, at the office.

It is very rude for an employer to call an employee freely at home except under extremely pressing circumstances or when the person's job requires it. It is unreasonable for most people to make their home hours an extension of the workday. I heard an executive tell a younger executive once that his time belonged to the company, and that included *all* his time. This is pure madness, of course. A company buys your services, not your entire life. There is very little business that can't be handled during the normal workweek, and it is rude to interfere with a person's private hours for anything less than an emergency.

9

WINING, DINING, AND DECLINING

THE BUSINESS LUNCH has been an integral part of corporate growth ever since God told Abraham over a midday meal that his wife was going to have a baby. In recent times the business lunch has become much less of an opportunity to do business than to cultivate goodwill. In some cases it is a way to sow the seeds of bad feeling. Many people no longer see breaking bread together as having any particular business value. People would rather spend their lunch hours shopping or going to the gym than meeting with some stranger for an expensive, tense meal.

Many executives refuse to accept invitations for business lunches, preferring to do business in a corporate setting or over the phone. Nonetheless, it is still a grand institution and very useful for some people.

Business lunches are generally nice gestures made by nice people who want to get to know you better in a graceful way for the long business haul and don't have any time to socialize during the workday. Other people use them rather shamefully. I know of one writer who would call publicity people every Monday and tell them what day of that week to take him to lunch.

Every good thing has its abusers, but in the main, lunch with the right person can be a very happy experience, not just with clients but with co-workers as well. The thing to remember is that for some people combining mealtimes with business is a very unnerving experience. Lunch is a time when personal good manners are on parade, and every little correction your mother gave you at the table as a kid comes into subconscious play. I had a wonderful business relationship with a young, beautifully mannered woman over a long period of time. In the office she was tact, grace, and charm—and self-confidence. At our first business lunch, she was shy, stumbling—but still charming—and tense. She kept telling me how much she liked the food, but I had the feeling that she never tasted much of it.

THE INVITE

When inviting someone to lunch, be sure you have a legitimate reason to do so and are prepared to pick up the check.

The unspoken rule is that no business lunch should ever be called unless there is a specific business reason for meeting—even if that reason is to cultivate goodwill and get to know an associate in a nonbusiness setting.

One woman editor complained to me that her pet peeve is that agents will call her and ask her to lunch. At lunch, she will politely wait for a business reason to come up, and usually there is none. Then there will be a long wait for her "host" to pick up the check. "Finally, because I am either bored with sitting or because I must get back to the office, I'll pay the check myself. Then I'll be angry with myself for doing it."

The problem of who pays the check is actually not a problem at all. The person who makes the invitation is the one who pays. A guest may insist on picking up the check, if he wants; but in every other case, the inviter pays.

CANCELING

It is acceptable to cancel a business lunch the same morning of the date. Business crises do arise that must take precedence. The person who cancels is the one responsible for rescheduling, although the original host will remain the host and still pick up the check. Two cancellations are not uncommon, but canceling three times is an indication that you don't want to have lunch unless you say otherwise.

There are times when bad weather is a reason for canceling a lunch date. The way to do this is to call your guest or host and ask if it would be convenient to reschedule, and cite the weather as a reason. Always make it clear that you will keep the date if it is not feasible to reschedule, but if both agree to cancel, then all is well.

If you are ill you may have a secretary cancel for you, but you must get back to the person at the earliest date to reschedule or apologize for not being able to get together at all.

LATE ONES

It is not polite to be late for a business lunch, since it is in effect a business meeting. It is especially bad to be late if you are the host. Whatever the reason for lateness, they should be good ones, and explained quickly to the person who was kept waiting. Then the matter should be dropped. If you are both late, thank each other and go eat.

There is still a thing called fashionably late. It is never stylish to be late just to be late for the business lunch or dinner. Fashion should be saved for social occasions. In business, try to be on time.

AT THE RESTAURANT

People usually meet at the restaurant for business lunches even when they have never met before. It is polite for the host to try to be there a few minutes early, especially if the guest is a new face and/or has never been to the restaurant before. There is another reason as well: this gives you an opportunity to have both coats checked together, since, as host, it is your responsibility to pay the coat check.

It is not polite to have your guest arrive by himself or herself and have to wait at the bar or at the table until you arrive. The reason for this is that the guest must take your lead in ordering and should not be required to wait nursing a drink until you arrive. Perhaps the guest doesn't drink hard liquor but will want wine for lunch; he or she is then left playing with the tablecloth. It is very awkward to wait alone in a restaurant for a person; you can't do anything but fiddle with your water glass.

If you are unavoidably detained, try to call the restaurant and have the maître d' cosset the guest for you. If this is impossible, apologize on arrival and play the rest out gracefully.

AT THE BAR

If you are waiting for someone for lunch, you may be seated at the bar until the companion arrives. If you have a drink there, the bar bill can be added to the lunch check. Some restaurants do not transfer bar tabs to lunch checks, and for these places you should carry some cash to cover the drinks quickly. It is necessary to leave a cash tip for the bartender in such a case. Guests as well as hosts may tell the bartender to add the bill to the lunch check. The tip for the bartender is then figured into the waiter's tip or added and indicated in a separate line on the check.

PREPPING THE MAÎTRE D'

If a restaurant is new to you, take the maître d' aside and ask him to be sure the check is brought to you, not your guest. If you are a woman, this is especially important, since many waiters will still present the check to the male and this can create a moment of embarrassment at the end of the lunch. A waiter should know that the person who orders the wine, or asks for the check, is the host, but unfortunately one cannot always count on a knowledgeable waiter.

It may be difficult for certain people in certain situations to take the back seat when they are guests for lunch. If the guest is a fifty-year-old executive and he is being taken out by a twenty-eight-year-old woman executive, he will always *appear* to be the host. Waiters will automatically bring him the check, defer to him, give him the wine list. The maître d' will greet him, not her, as they enter. She will appear somewhat presumptuous when she takes the lead each time someone asks him something, but she must play out the role.

The best thing to do is to make sure the reservations are in her name—her full name—or in Miss Somebody's name. If the woman arrives early, she can make it clear by her presence that she is paying and should be treated as host. Women execs are well served by choosing certain restaurants and becoming regular patrons so there will not be this kind of confusion. If there is one place where women have had a long-standing reputation of paying for the man, it is at business lunches. But you can't always get through to some people.

Also, if you eat regularly at a restaurant, you may arrange to have yourself billed monthly and just sign for the check.

WHERE THE TAB STOPS

The business lunch does bring out whole throngs of people who are secretly looking for a treat. It should be remembered all through soup to dessert that none of this should ever be considered a free meal. The purpose of a business lunch is to promote business in some way. By trying to use it as a party or a freebie, you can jeopardize your own professional reputation and put an unwelcome strain on someone else's expense account.

One woman in the fashion industry is well known for inviting people to lunch, then blithely ignoring the bill until the other person picks it up. Since she has an expense account, she has a bad reputation for this practice. Someone finally got even. When the bill was about to be presented, he got up from his seat and said, "It's been delightful talking to you, but I have another appointment and I'm late." He walked out quickly, leaving her with the check.

To prevent their guests from having any possibility of a moment's doubt or discomfort, some people never allow a check to be brought to the table. They make arrangements for the tip and bill with the maître d' beforehand, so the smoothness of the lunch atmosphere need not be halted while a check is figured and paid in silence. This is more style and elegance than etiquette, but if it can be arranged, nothing can be more impressive.

Why all this fuss about a check? Everyone knows that the meal is going to have to be paid for and that tips to waiters must be figured. It is not explainable, but as soon as a check is brought to the table after a meal there is always a moment's silence. It is a conversation-stopper even when there is no doubt about who is paying. Anything that smoothes the moment should be done.

The best way to handle a check is to handle it apart from the table. It helps to have an account so you can just sign the check and leave a standard tip so there will be no addition at the table. It can all be checked later at the office when the bill is sent. Credit cards also help smooth things.

The worst way is to use money. It is clumsy and the flash of cold cash is a psychological jolt. Also, there it is in plain sight to see: how much you're paying and how much you're tipping. The guest can't look away and can't look at what you're doing.

GOING DUTCH

There are only two rules to going dutch: split the check fairly, and don't take the check stub for your own expense account if you aren't paying the whole bill.

When lunching with co-workers of varying incomes, be sure that you *don't* split the check evenly unless it really turns out that way. A young person making two hundred dollars a week can't pay part of the bill for someone else who makes twice that much and has had several drinks to boot. If someone has not had any drinks, split the food bill; then the drinkers add the bar bill and pay the difference.

214 — THE NEW OFFICE ETIQUETTE

Drinkers should also pay a larger share of the tip since their bill has increased the amount of the check.

CHECKING EXTRAVAGANCE

It is good manners for the host at a business lunch to signal the guest when there is a need to limit the cost of the bill. Some guests will brazenly ask the waiter to bring extra bottles of wine or order expensive wines and extra drinks through lunch without asking the host if they may. It is a terrible imposition and very rude to spend someone else's money without permission.

A host has the right to cut short the lunch in this case or to halt the order of extras by saying, "I'm afraid I am running late," or, "I must keep the lunch short this time because we have a meeting back at the office." Some hosts will actually request the check from the waiter early to save time.

The host should order first, or suggest certain items to the guest, to indicate the price range of the lunch. Don't order an appetizer unless urged to do so, and if the host suggests wine, let him or her order it. Dessert and follow-ups on martinis are ordered if offered, or if the host orders more.

If there is no limit on what can be ordered, the host should say, "I am not sure I will have much, but please order whatever you're in the mood for," or, "I'm very hungry today. I hope you are, too."

If the host defers to your wine judgment, ask point-blank if there is a ceiling on the cost of the wine. In this case the host should say what the range is.

THE DRY WELL

Some people who have their expense accounts cut may try to keep up appearances by continuing to spend as much and bearing the cost (which is foolish) or by dropping out of sight through embarrassment. There is nothing wrong with communicating a cutback to standard lunch guests. The best thing to do is say that although your expense account has been limited drastically, you would like to continue the relationship—but you are not able to pick up the tab regularly anymore.

People who truly care about the lunches as a part of their business will understand and offer to share or even to pay for some of the lunches. In business everyone knows the state of the economy, and if your own budget has been cut, you can be sure that almost every other company is doing the same. The nice thing about socializing with friends in your own field is you are all in the same economic boat together. No pretenses need stand in the way of proper business socializing.

PROCEDURE

There is no reason to rush your guest through lunch unless he or she is acting badly or is becoming very drunk and may make an embarrassing scene. Take your time through drinks, if you are drinking, and have the waiter wait until you call him to order your meal. I once planned on having a leisurely meal in a quiet restaurant, *très* small and properly intimate for us two old business friends who hadn't seen each other in years.

My guest had to catch a plane in a few hours, and we planned on a long lunch. We ordered drinks and were asked if we wanted to order our meal. We figured that it would take twenty minutes to get what we wanted, and the waiter agreed. So we ordered and started to unwind.

Halfway through the first drink the food arrived. We commented on the speed of the delivery—so rare these days. The waiter smiled as if he had done a good deed, then remembered. He asked if we wanted it kept warm in the kitchen, a prospect that caused my guest to go green under her tan. We ate, and the waiter brought the check. It seemed the place closed at 2:00, and here were were: 2:05. There was nothing to do but drive to the airport early and watch the jet fumes from an orange-and-red plastic cocktail bar. So much for the special reunion.

Always check out the restaurant before making reservations. Ask the price range of the entrees, the hours of service, the closeness of the tables—and hope for the best. Any planning you can do in advance will ease your job in the restaurant and make you better able to enjoy the meal, which is the whole point of it in the first place.

PERSONAL NEEDS

Some people view certain biological functions or mention of them at the table as somewhat unmannerly. They go to great pains and embarrassments to blow their noses discreetly, and they become embarrassed at having to excuse themselves to go to the rest room.

There is nothing out of order in doing either. Many times the atmosphere of a restaurant, redolent of cuisine and cigarette smoke, or the eating of hot, spicy foods causes stimulation of the sinuses. This creates a need to use a handkerchief or tissue. Do it without thinking about it. I have seen perfectly charming, beautifully mannered people try to blow their noses without actually doing it. They dab lightly and discreetly and make themselves uncomfortable.

I have also seen grown men and women—more often men— blush when they excuse themselves to go to the rest room. Women are more practical about such matters. Although it usually would be rude to belch loudly at the table, certain normal bodily functions are respected by everyone. In some areas of the country it would not even be offensive to belch after a meal.

TIPPING

Tipping is an important part of the lunch etiquette. The fact that Americans tip extremely well surprises many European visitors to our luncheon shores, since overseas tips are usually reckoned in coins, whereas here they are computed in paper bills. The current tipping percentage rate dictates that one leave 15 percent of the total amount of the lunch bill to the waiter. This is computed on the untaxed amount, not the final figure, unless you wish to be generous. In New York the tax on a lunch bill is 8 percent, so the custom there is to double the tax and give it to the waiter. That provides a 16 percent tip, which is generous. If there is no tax or the tax in your state is less or more, then you will have to learn to compute it on your own.

Other tips, such as for the captain or maître d' and for the sommelier (wine captain), are computed at 7 percent of the untaxed bill or one half the amount of the waiter's tip, whichever you prefer. Tips for a checkroom may range from twenty-five cents to one dollar. If you are tipping twenty-five cents, make sure it is for each person whose possessions are checked. This tip is not given with the other tips. All tips to waiter, sommelier, and maître d' are left at the table or on the credit card.

THE COATROOM

Although many people are not aware of it, during a business lunch the host picks up all the costs of everything charged for in the restaurant. This includes all the drinks—even if the guest arrived somewhat early and had a drink at the bar—and whatever fee or tip is required at the coat-check room. If the guest is holding his or her coat check, the host should ask for it after the meal and then present both his and the guest's to the person at the coatroom. The host pays as well as helping the guest with the wraps if help is necessary.

SEPARATING AFTER THE MEAL

Some people feel it is gracious to help the guest obtain a cab and see him or her safely off before separating. Others go so far as to pay for the cost of the cab, although, unless you are also taking the same cab, it would be wrong to offer cash to a guest. Presumably, the guest can pay for the cab if he gets in it. If you are taking a cab yourself, you can always ask if you can drop the guest at a destination that is on the way. If it takes you out of your way, the guest should defer. Your responsibility ends when you leave the restaurant.

If you both work in the same area and are heading back to the office, it is always nice to walk awhile with the guest. If you are in a hurry, though, there is no need for this.

RUDENESS BECOMES A FAST EXIT

When a guest at lunch becomes a boor, the best approach is to pull out the "I-have-a-meeting" excuse and bring the lunch to an end as quickly as possible. Boorish behavior can encompass anything from loudness, embarrassing remarks to the waiter, or overordering to outright nastiness. Drunkenness is also a species of boorish behavior, but it requires special treatment and will be discussed later as an emergency.

One person whose career was partly made up of regular business lunches said he usually would apologize to his boorish guest and say, "I'm sorry, but I have to get back to the office . . . the big boss called a meeting this morning and it started already. Why don't you stay and finish the wine or have desert and I'll leave."

Then he would pay the check and leave the boor to be boorish alone.

There is no reason to sit through a lunch with a rude person any longer than is necessary. If it becomes obvious you are being used for a free lunch and no business will come of it, or if the rudeness is such that it embarrasses you, then skip dessert and coffee, pay the check, and get away as quickly as possible. It does no good to be rude in return, but you can be swift and detach yourself from the guest as soon as is decently possible. Remember, the reason for the business lunch always is to do business in some way. There is no reason to waste any more time at a fruitless lunch than you would on a crank phone call.

NONDRINKERS

I do not like to drink during the day, even if I am not returning to work. If I am working, alcohol eliminates any possibility of functioning efficiently. At a business lunch, though, the time spent over the drink is essential to warming up the conversation. The host usually wants a drink, since the pressure is on him or her. Since I am usually a guest, I try to order something like a Perrier, a virgin mary, juice, or a Campari and soda, whether or not I want one. I actually dislike all of these potables, but people who want to drink usually become very uncomfortable if you are not at least nursing something in a glass. Out of consideration for my host I always order something wet.

I was once told that it is rude to order coffee before or during a meal because the distinctive aroma spoils the palate of the people at the table and hinders their enjoyment of the food. I agree, but an early lunch can often excuse the request for a coffee instead of a drink if one has not yet had time for breakfast. Such a choice is not elegant, but it is not rude, either. In any event, the cigarette smoke in most restaurants cancels out the taste buds of everyone in the room.

AVOIDING LUNCH

As mentioned earlier, many people hate to go to business lunches, and it is not hard to see why. The conversation is stilted; no one is very relaxed; there is too much protocol to make digestion a pleasant pastime. I find business lunches somewhat draining because they last too long, generally require eating food that is best eaten at dinner, and are too much of a production for the middle of the workday.

One top executive refuses to accept lunch invitations. He says, "I want to do business with you, and I enjoy it and will continue to do so as long as we serve each other's needs. But I don't want you to

220 — THE NEW OFFICE ETIQUETTE

feel that taking me to lunch—or even inviting me—every so often will make any difference to our relationship. So I must decline."

Many people consider the business lunch a waste of time and an ordeal, just as many see it as an elegant and enjoyable pleasure that enhances the art of working for a living. The choice is yours. Many companies require some of their personnel to turn in a certain number of expense vouchers for business lunches each month, or they question them on it. Others realize that it seldom makes any difference.

SMALL TALK

The stylish gossip among people in the same general field of business usually is based on a certain amount of cattiness and viciousness. The jokes in vogue at any given time among executives of any business are usually too biting or ethnic or politically rabid to be used as small talk with a stranger.

The best warm-ups are usually stories that are semipersonal or deal with the state of the economy and how one's business is faring in relation to it, or friendly personal getting-to-know-you questions about marital status (acceptable here), where one worked before, and possible common acquaintances.

My favorite lunch talk has always been to hear my host, usually a perfect stranger, tell me about his co-op and how much he wants to sell it for. It's a nice warm-up, makes me jealous as hell, and adds a nice intimate friendliness to lunch. I generally want to counter with how much I realized when I pawned my watch to pay for the cab that took me to lunch, but I never do.

Small talk should never get into ethnic subjects, unless you are both of the same background; politics, except to talk about how they affect your business; and certainly not religion, since these days top-level execs are doing things spiritually that are more controversial than Catholic, Protestant, or Jew. Anything in the news is all right; so is the show or movie that's a must to see, the cost of housing, and kids. Otherwise, get to know the person better before telling the latest joke about the latest minority group.

WHEN THE ALCOHOL HITS

It happens at times that in the pressure of getting to lunch and unwinding, the drink or two that you used as a relaxer hits a little too hard. It is important at that time to *say* that the alcohol caused too much of a buzz and order some coffee quickly. It would be worse to make a fool of yourself, speak with a slurred tongue, or break a glass. Everyone knows how liquor or wine can hit at that time of day. Don't play games with it. Be straightforward and get the thing cleared up. There can be nothing more unattractive than stumbling out of a restaurant because you're drunk.

EMERGENCIES

Should an illness or a choking or extreme drunkenness occur at the table, the lunch is automatically ended. Call for the check, pay it, and slip the maître d' an extra bill for his help.

Small emergencies can be handled without stopping the lunch, however. If you should have a nosebleed or a coughing or sneezing fit, excuse yourself, assure the host you can handle it, and head for the rest room. If it goes on too long, ask a restaurant employee to inform your companion either that you are all right or that you must leave. But don't return to the table unless you are composed.

If you have had to interrupt a lunch because of a companion's drunkenness, do not mention the incident again. You are under an obligation to make sure the drunken person gets somewhere safely, but it is taken for granted that things were all right later. Don't embarrass him or her by referring to it. If it seems that it could happen again, find some other way to do business with the person.

If a person became ill at lunch, you should check the next day to be sure all is well. If it isn't, flowers or a card should be sent.

If the person was a choking victim—and lived—be sure to concern yourself with a follow-up. This is in the same category as an accident and is not a matter for embarrassment.

YOUR REPUTATION

Be careful whom you take to your favorite restaurant. You may be a regular client there, but the owners have a right not to have drunkenness or embarrassing situations occur on their premises. Establish yourself with the staff, including the bartender, and you will never have to worry about your guests if you are late. They will be seated at your table and taken care of as if you were there.

BLOW OFF

It sometimes happens that restaurant tables are set close together and people at the next table are in essence forced to share the atmosphere with you. This can be irritating if someone at the next table eats noisily, smokes, has bad manners, or is loud.

I was told of one incident where a publicity man took an executive to lunch and they were placed almost touching the table of the people next to them. The woman at the next table resented their presence and started blowing cigarette smoke their way. The guest of the publicity man asked her to please aim the smoke away. The host was embarrassed and thought to soften the request by saying, "He just quit smoking and the smoke is a problem."

The woman smiled sourly and said, "There's nothing worse than an ex-smoker." The executive reddened and retorted to her, "Oh, I think there are a few things that are worse . . . yes, there are a few things."

The publicity man at his table and the woman's companion at theirs immediately started talking to head off an incident, and since they were finished eating, the man called for the check and they left as quickly as possible.

There would have been no polite way to stop the argument if it had continued. By repeatedly interjecting to save the day by changing the conversation back to himself, the publicity man was asking for his guest's cooperation, and got it, to avoid a scene. The guest should simply have let the matter lie and not bothered to retort to the woman, despite her blatant rudeness. In such a situation, where people are eating, whatever must be left unsaid to prevent an ugly scene should be. Ego must be set aside.

THE POACHERS

The situation sometimes arises in a restaurant that someone—often a friend—is listening in on your conversation. If the person is a stranger and is sitting looking and listening, the only approach is to stop midway in a sentence as if you are trying to think of something and stare at the person intently until he turns away and minds his own business. This can also be used on a friend, but if a friend is listening, it is an act of rudeness on his part, and it is not likely he will be able not to pay attention to your talk.

In this case the best thing to do is change the subject, telling your companion that perhaps you had better pursue the conversation in more private surroundings. If the talk is about something that must be discussed, speak in lower tones or suggest that you adjourn to the bar, or to your office if it is handy and nearby.

If the poacher actually tries to join you or tries to maintain a conversation across the tables, just say, "Excuse me, but we have to talk about a project, and this is the only time we can get together. Let's get on the phone later and we can talk."

Rudeness in a restaurant is one of the most difficult situations to deal with, since you cannot be rude in return, and any sort of effective put-down either will cause a scene that cannot be ignored by other diners or will make you look very bad, too.

This brings up another point about dining in public. You cannot control all conditions. People do smoke, laugh, talk loudly, and relax. If the general tone of the clientele is elegant, these activities are naturally subdued. If you are in a place where newsmen hang out, the place will not be as quiet as a "little-old-lady restaurant." Don't make a fuss over certain things that are acceptable behavior, even if they bother you momentarily. If the noise or smoke makes a travesty of conversation or breathing, then either leave or ask the people to cool it. If they do—and they probably won't really be able to—fine; if not, cut the meal short and go back to the office for the rest of the business talk. Next time eat at a different restaurant. Also, apologize to your guest when you leave the restaurant and thank him for his patience. This reaffirms to both of you that you recognized uncontrollable circumstances, and it did not affect your relationship adversely. Sharing such things, in fact, strengthens the bonds of friendship. Like going through hell week together.

THAT'S ENTERTAINMENT

Many people enjoy entertaining the people they work with at home or elsewhere. For many people the invitation to a co-worker's home is an occasion for inner groaning. Others like the idea and see it as a treat. The general rule about entertaining at home for business reasons is to make sure that it is never presented as an obligation. Also, try to have some valid reason besides pure socializing for a party.

ENTERTAINING THE BOSS

Whenever you plan to socialize with your boss, remember these things:

- Do not invite him to your place alone unless you already have an easy rapport with him. Dinner at home is no time to try to establish such an interaction.
- Be sure that you want to do this sort of thing on a continuing basis. Inviting the boss to socialize indicates that there is a possibility of cultivating a relationship that is an addition to the one in the office.

The pressure of inviting one's boss to one's home is rather heavy. You want to impress him or her favorably, yet you don't want to seem to be living frivolously beyond your means. Remember that the one person who knows exactly how much you make is the person you work for. He does not expect you to entertain beyond your means. Just because the boss has a large salary does not mean that it is a condescension to enjoy eating a meal served on your coffee table in your small apartment. It is always the approach you take as a host that makes the evening worthwhile. Don't make empty gestures beyond your means.

If you are a highly paid executive, at the same level basically as your boss, there is no reason not to serve the best money can buy. If you care enough to invite your boss, don't be cheap about it.

Never invite your boss strictly because you feel it will advance your career. There are too many other avenues open which are less likely to fail. Invite the boss home only if you genuinely have a warm relationship and want to expand it.

I heard a story of one highly paid airline executive who was building a summer house at the beach. His boss had a place nearby and expressed a desire to see his when it was completed. As soon as that time arrived, the exec invited his boss over for drinks and dinner. The boss arrived and saw that most of the place had been furnished with the same items that were used in the company's VIP room at the airport. Since the man was in charge of ordering the furniture, it was obvious that he had just ordered extra for his new house. The boss enjoyed drinks and dinner and went back to the office on Monday and fired him.

It seems odd that anyone so far up in the corporate structure should have done anything so incredibly stupid, but there are many people who advance through niceness, not through intelligence.

Other people are smart enough to carry off the most outrageous things and never run into any flak. I knew one gay man who invited his boss and his wife to go camping in the tropics with him and his male lover. The company paid for the trip since it was part of the business. When entertaining your boss you can basically carry off any sort of supposed no-no if you do it with the proper style, grace, and savvy.

IF YOU CAN'T COOK

When entertaining at home, don't do the cooking yourself unless you know how to cook well. People become bored with having to go through a series of bad meals in silence just to avoid hurting your feelings. Ask a trusted friend to tell you the truth. I had an Italian-American friend who always was having co-workers in for home-cooked Italian meals. They were awful, and everyone hated to go because she just couldn't cook.

Gourmet stores are wonderful places to shop if you are not a good cook. The cost of buying there seems expensive only on the surface. When buying enough for two or three, it is not only affordable but impressive—and the food already cooked. If you are a lost lamb in such a shop, remember the man or woman behind the counter can tell you exactly which paté goes with which quiche and, even further, can suggest the right kind of wine to go with it. Everything from the hors d'oeuvres to the dessert can be purchased here—even the special coffee blend. Things are generally sold by the quarter or half pound, so you can buy exactly enough for each person and save money.

I find that anything that is already prepared on the day of the dinner makes it that much easier to be a good host. Don't wear yourself into a frazzle after work getting things at the last minute. A dinner for the boss should be planned far enough in advance and with the same businesslike approach as you would any other company activity. Always shop the day before; wash the lettuce, get the flowers, choose the wine, and make sure the Scotch and gin bottles are full.

Always make sure the house is clean, even if you are sparse on furniture or making do until you get fully settled in. Real elegance in entertaining comes from your accepting your own style and remembering that, in your house, you set the tone for the evening. Don't try to imitate something else that you think may be better. If there is any place you must not apologize for yourself, it is your own home.

Ask people ahead of time what they dislike and what they can't eat before extending an invitation. It may be better to have some people in for drinks or parties rather than dinner.

Don't invite more than three people home unless you plan on a more general party invitation. It is best to invite singles or only two people at a time to avoid slighting some people at the office. People may wonder why they are not included in the group if it looks like an office party.

FRIENDS AND BUTLERS

When entertaining business people at a large party at home, it is probably a good idea to hire some help. A bartender or a butler takes the pressure off you, makes a nice impression, and is tax-deductible. Often it helps to use friends who need the money, since they can be more reliable than strangers.

Bartenders do make some people feel uncomfortable. People who feel insecure often cannot deal well with "servants." If you're a guest, treat bartenders and butlers the way you treat anyone else at the party, but don't interfere with their work by engaging them in conversation. It is also not likely the butler or bartender can answer certain questions about the house, the paintings, or the cut-glass punch bowl that looks like an heirloom. Limit your remarks to the help to ordering your drinks and accepting or refusing the canapés.

Don't play games with the bartender. One friend of mine who moonlights as a party bartender was subjected to one man who came up and started making comments about the host's co-op and how much it cost. The bartender offered no remarks, and the man turned and said, "I'm with the German embassy!" Indeed he was, but the bartender didn't really care. All he wanted to know was what kind of drink he liked.

Butlers and bartenders are paid and should not be tipped by the guests; neither should any servant at a party. The host does tip, and the amount can be lavish if the service is superspecial. If the bartender leaves your whole kitchen clean, for example, a fifteen- or twenty-dollar tip is not crass. That amount is above the set fee.

THE NERVOUS MATE

When inviting people from the office to your home for a social gathering, be sure that you actually *want* them there. Many very fine executives go through their whole careers well respected and liked by their personnel and never let them within ten blocks of the house. No one needs a day in your backyard or on your terrace. It may even be considered an imposition or seen as a duty or requirement.

If you are married or living with someone, make sure you have the willing cooperation of this person before filling the house with throngs of strangers. Few things are more detrimental to the goodwill you want to engender than a spouse or mate pulling a long face and making snide remarks to your co-workers and boss in your home. It is expected from a spouse that he or she will cohost an office party in the home; an unmarried mate is not expected to do this unless the relationship is based on such sharing.

If you do extend an invitation, do not take the attitude that your visitors are there for an ulterior reason. Treat them as your honored guests, not as people you have to throw largesse to. Some people are very private about their homes and do not like strangers in the house. If your mate is such a person, respect his or her nervousness and keep the office away.

I was told a story of one top executive of a small company who invited his staff home one Saturday afternoon. It was a hot day, and it required a long ride to get there for most people. They were taken around back into the yard where the food and drink were to be served. There was not a large variety of either, but the bad moment came when one woman asked to use the bathroom. The hostess froze. It was evident she had never considered that anyone would actually be going inside the house.

The guest was sent in anyway, and while she was in the bathroom, freshening herself because of the heat, she heard the boss's wife coming through the upstairs hall saying, "Fran. . . ? Where are you?"

Fran answered in a loud voice that she was in the bathroom, but it was evident that the hostess was checking to see that Fran was not rifling the jewelry box.

If you don't want people in, don't invite them. If you do, you must trust them and open your house to them. If you want certain rooms off limits, close the doors. It is usually a good idea to leave one bedroom open, in case someone feels faint or if that is where the coats are kept. Certainly bear in mind that people use the bathroom during a party and use it often.

WHOM TO INVITE

When planning any sort of business entertaining at home, it is best to carefully consider the people who are coming. It is not, for example, a good idea to have the known office lush come alone or with one or two others for dinner. He or she will start drinking on and on and you may end up finally having to get a cab around one in the morning after a very trying, embarrassing evening. Invite drunks to large parties, when someone can cart the soused guests home for you.

It is, of course, bad manners to become passing-out drunk at a co-worker's home, but it happens. All you can do is try to control the way it happens so you won't end up with a large, limp deadweight on the couch.

It is often a good idea to invite close friends in to mix with business associates. They generally are helpful during the party, fetching ice and other items you may run out of. They can help move things along smoothly. When having only folks from the office, it is permissible to have personal friends in as well, but only if there is a possibility that they will fit in. The best time to mix friends and business is when the business people are not all from your own company.

SECRET LOVES

We all have little secrets—embarrassing or not—we don't want to share with the office. It may be something as simple as the fact that we like to paint as a hobby but are modest about it, or the fact that we like to wear jackboots and panty hose around the house and be photographed that way. It's always best to scout the house for the porno that fell under the footstool, the picture of your niece at the skinny-dip party, or the insurance policy made out to your dear old mother in Albany. Whatever you don't want to share, hide where no one has a right to look or where it won't be accidentally uncovered by taking a book off the shelf.

I had one friend who had some books that belonged to his father. He had never opened them, but there were some embarrassing pictures stuck in between the leaves of some. They were discovered about five minutes before the bulk of the guests arrived by an early arrival who had been asked to entertain himself.

As a guest, it is best not to examine anything without first asking permission. The rare Stradivarius on the piano may be damaged if you touch it. The host may not like people going through his possessions. Don't assume that everything in the house is open to inspection. You are invited for a party, not for an appraisal.

SETTING THE LIMITS

When having a dinner party or a large gathering at your house, you cannot politely set limits on the time your guests may stay. You must plan to devote your entire evening to the entertainment, even if some people hang on and on. If one person is laying over past a reasonable time, you can say, "Let me walk you out to your car," or, "Let me get a cab for you, since it's getting pretty late to be walking alone outside." I knew one experienced party-giver who would actually ask certain people who were leaving to see if they could give a lift to people who were going their way. This took a great deal of style, and no one was ever offended. And no one was ever left in the house after 11:15 P.M.

A cocktail party may go on until 11:00 P.M. if people are having a good time. If you want them to clear out early, invite them after work for cocktails until eight, and tell the butler, if there is one, to start cleaning up at that time. People are required to watch the time if the host has set a limit to the party.

One host I knew would invite people in for drinks "before dinner" and make a point of saying several times throughout that he and his wife were meeting someone for dinner at a certain hour. It worked, since people were aware that it was a cocktail party only and prepared themselves to leave at a proper time.

EMBARRASSING SITUATIONS

I have seen it happen that two people who are attracted to each other will go into the bathroom together and lock the door at business parties, or go into the bedroom to be alone to watch TV together on the coats. This is rude, of course, and the latter innocent conduct is probably the more rude. If you want to watch TV, go home. At a co-worker's home, you are invited to participate in the socializing. If you don't want to, you can decline the invitation.

It is also rude for guests at a party to indulge their romantic appetites in the bathroom, bedroom, or broom closet of a co-worker's home. Sensual trysting can be carried out at any number of motels on the way home instead, without preventing other people from making more legitimate use of the bathroom facilities. Some people become extremely enraged at having others use their homes for sex, seeing it as an insult and a desecration of the hearth, so to speak. It is in fact worse than rude to let one's animal passion go out of control on the spot and make what may be termed a pig of oneself at a party.

ANIMALS

Your beloved dog, cat, or parrot is likely to become high-strung, angry, or obnoxious at a party. Unless your animals are used to people, try not to include them in the party proper. If you can take the puppy to a friend's place for the duration of the party, it is best to do so. Cats are generally able to hide themselves adequately if they hate parties. But birds should be covered so they do not become upset. One friend of mine had a parrot that he kept on a perch. The bird hated strangers, although they were fascinated by him. They would come up to make friends, and he would get on their hand, walk up their arm, sit on their shoulder, get on top of their head, and take hold of the ear painfully and not let go. If your animal likes blood, keep him caged.

Pets should not be permitted to beg from guests unless the guests are old friends of the animal. In a business situation, keep the pets away from the table so your guest can relax. He didn't come to feed your dog; he came to eat. Overnight guests should not have to sleep with your animals, nor should they have to play fetch, stroke them for hours, or go home covered with fur and feathers unless they wore them when they came in. Animals are best shared with friends who love them almost as much as you do. Keep them off the corporate lap.

10

NEW WAVES
AND FREE AGENTS

THE FACE OF business has changed to the point where free-lanc-ers have become a large and integral sideline of regular company staff people. Free-lancers may take part in making decisions along with staff personnel; in some cases, they may even make decisions for staffers to follow. Obviously there is some new etiquette in-volved in dealing with these situations, since many of them did not exist in business before five years ago.

MUTUAL DEADLINES

All free-lance people are given a deadline for their work to be submitted. If you use free-lance people, remember that they proba-bly are in no financial position to wait indefinitely to receive their money. Deadlines are mutual; companies should provide guaran-tees that checks will be sent out within thirty days of receipt of ma-terial, just as they must with any material supplier. If a free-lancer must wait long past the expected time for payment, he actually

233

does not realize that money because his budget is torpedoed and he must find some way to borrow the money. This leads to a hand-to-mouth existence and is not feasible.

Companies have begun the practice of hanging on to money owed as long as possible to realize more daily interest on their money, but this is actually using someone else's money to gain interest once the date of payment is past.

DRESSING TO MEET

Free agents should be aware that if they are working for a company briefly, they are representing that company for that time and should try to make their appearance coincide with the company image. Their behavior is also important and should not reflect badly on the company. To throw temper tantrums, to fling the company name about as one's own to gain some temporary clout—all this is bad business.

Any work done for a company should be accompanied with respect for the company image, for the person who has given you the assignment, and for the fact that you will want to establish yourself favorably for future work.

If you are to meet with higher-level executives, don't show up in Levi's and tennis shoes, even if that is the apparel of the people in the office in general. Do not take things for granted. Always try to keep your image one-up when meeting certain personnel for the first time. If their attitude is relaxed and they welcome you as one of the company, then on future visits you can be as casual as they are. If they expect some kind of care in clothes, then you are safe. You can never offend by being well dressed or well groomed. No matter what the weather, never appear at a place of business in shorts or a halter top.

ATTITUDES

If you dislike the corporate structure, that is your affair. Do not put a company down by manner or attitude while on its turf.

It is important to respect the fact that a company's leisure times may not coincide with yours. If you stop in to see a staff person at a company, do not bring your companions into the office with you. Leave your friends in the reception area, and don't take up too much time. Some clients welcome the diversion when the day is slow and will ask you to hang out for a while. Unless specifically asked, make your visit brief and to the point. And friendly. It is possible to be concise and friendly at the same time.

Although it is necessary from a public-relations point of view for free-lancers to visit their clients in a friendly way even when not on business, make sure you call first to set up a visit, and don't drop in unexpectedly. The goodwill is engendered only through your clients being happy to see you.

EXPENSES

Always check with your contact before making expenses on assignment. There may be ways to make long-distance phone calls without having to put in a voucher. One editor of mine has me bill his line direct when I call from my house to save time and trouble.

On the other hand, it is not necessary to put yourself through a great deal of added time and hassle just to save a few dollars for the company. Certain expenses are expected at times. If you must fly to another town and carry equipment, it is reasonable to expect to have the cab or car paid for by the company, as well as assistant's expenses. If you must rise early to catch a plane, then again a cab is essential. If it is convenient to take less expensive transportation, then you should do so, but not if it means an unreasonable amount of effort and time expended.

It is generally expected that the assigner company will pay for all expenses incurred on a trip you make for it. This includes meals, phone calls, accommodations, and transportation. When you work in town, however, meals, some transportation, and local calls are not billed.

In most cases, the company should provide a cash advance if the expenses are expected to be over one hundred dollars. The company must be responsible for accidents incurred on assignment if the accident was a direct result of the job. All expenses and liabilities should be cleared with the employer in advance.

GUARANTEES

Most free-lance assignments are taken on faith, but it should be requested that there be some sort of written document outlining fees, deadlines, and special considerations in case of a falling out or in case the assigning contact leaves his job and the company wants to default on the assignment. Generally it is acceptable that on default the company pays a "kill fee" to make up for the expenses incurred by the free agent.

If the assignment itself is to require a long outlay of time—three months to a year—by the free agent, then the company should pay half of the fee in advance. And in this case the company should be responsible for the entire fee even if the assignment is canceled.

If the company assigns a job and when the job is done decides not to use it, the company should pay the full fee. If a contract exists, this is a legal responsibility.

NEW CONTACTS

When scouting new contacts for your free-lance work, it is always best to query first by letter, then follow up with a phone call. If you have a recommendation from someone else, you can phone first and use that person's name. Never contact an employer without having several specific suggestions in mind that you think can be used by the company. Familiarize yourself with the company and its products, and do some research into what it has and has not done. Do not waste time asking the company to fill you in on its needs. Do not ask for free products to familiarize yourself with them so you can offer suggestions. This is highly unprofessional.

If you have something to sell, you must have the intelligence to gauge employers' needs. If you are unwilling to do any quality work in advance, do not waste their time getting a free ride.

These days, too, it is no longer acceptable to ask free agents to work on speculation. Direct assignments are the only proper way to ask a person to work for you, and the agreement of a kill fee is standard operating procedure. No free agent can afford the time and expense of speculative work.

Any client that assigns work and decides not to use it should pay the full amount, unless the free-lancer gets enough other work to permit a kill fee to be accepted. In any event, the free-lancer must be apprised of the situation immediately, and not just sent a kill fee without prior notification.

HOW MANY TIMES?

It is permitted to offer as many proposals to any company as you feel it can use. But you should try not to bug someone every day with every thought that comes off your head. Set up the kind of relationship that will enable you to know when and what to offer a client. Special "fast" projects that are requested from you and require you to set aside other work should bring a higher fee, unless the client provides you with so much work that this favor is something that is worth doing. You should not go out of your way for companies that do not reciprocate financially or with volume of free-lance work.

11

THE TRAVELING
BUSINESS

THERE COMES A time in business when you have to travel somewhere for the company. Sometimes these are actual business trips made alone; sometimes they are gatherings in a resort area for out-of-office business meetings or conventions. They're often fun, always free, and can be either horror stories or relaxation and recuperation.

The important thing to remember is that you must continue to comport yourself as an adult and a professional business person. Many people faced with the tension of spending four solid days captive in the same place with their co-workers become a little crazed—and a little frightened. Will I talk in my sleep? Will I get any sleep? Will I get enough to eat? Will I look silly in a bathing suit? What if the boss talks to me? What if he doesn't?

GETTING THERE

If you can travel to the place with someone who is close to you at the office, it is best to do so. This makes you feel more secure, whatever the trip is about. It also helps if the rooms have been assigned so that people who know each other will be rooming together. This doesn't make much difference, actually, since you won't be spending a lot of time in the room, but the psychology is there. I have found that evening gatherings in the rooms are more relaxed if you are with the people you would normally interact easily with at the office.

I once traveled on an early flight a day later than most of the others to such a meeting in Jamaica and shared the ride with my publisher. Up until that time I had liked him a lot. But he was so hyped up over the impending fun that he wouldn't stop talking—loudly—from the time we met at the airport VIP room in New York to the time we separated at the hotel in the tropics. The whole four-hour flight I sat in petrified silence listening to his bombast while he regaled me, the stewardesses, anyone who came in range with his quips and wit. By the time we landed I was unable to cope with reality and had totally clammed up. At the hotel I said I was going to sleep. He looked at me critically and said, "Boy, the tropical lassitude hits you fast, doesn't it?" I swerved into my room, not bothering to open the door first.

There should be a give-and-take here. Some people start having the party as soon as they leave the office; others prefer to be a little more subdued. The thing to remember is that you are going, ostensibly, on a free vacation with a little work. Most people see it as a blowout, sort of like New Year's Eve. Others would rather not go at all. The best approach is to be rowdy with the rowdies and let the quiet ones soak up the sun in peace.

CONGENIALITY

You're very much on view at conventions, and it's best to remember that you are, in effect, at work. You're working overtime, but it's still work. Try to keep good humor going, be more relaxed and social than at the office, but don't let your guard down. At one of these gatherings I once witnessed a loud argument at lunch on the veranda, and it embarrassed all the English business people who heard it. If you don't feel well, lie down in the sun or off somewhere. If you can, try to take part in some of what is passing for fun.

STRANGENESS

People may act strangely at such affairs. Once, I was talking to a close friend of mine on the hotel lawn and couldn't understand why he wasn't responding normally to simple conversation. While we—I—conversed, a young man came up and asked to speak to me about buying some drugs from him. He'd already sold some to others in the group, I gathered, which is why I was not getting predictable responses from my friend.

Drugs, drunkenness, and such are dangerous things to play with from a career point of view at these affairs. They may cut into your reputation with your boss or make you look foolish. I was told about one woman who predictably gets so drunk every night at conventions for the fashion industry that someone has to help her to her room. It is sad, and no one ever really talks about it, but she is well known as needing to have an escort at some point. The only polite thing to do is get her to her room and say good night and see her the next day, bright and cheery, and never mention it.

SEX IN THE MARKETPLACE

Something sexual comes to mind to many people when they think of going to a hotel for a convention. Perhaps it is the mystique of all those bedrooms lined up next to each other; perhaps it is the idea that all those people are captive roommates for that length of time. Perhaps it's race memory of early man's primitive rites of spring. Who knows? It happens.

The best course of action at a convention is to keep your sexuality in check. It should not be considered a time to put the make on that elusive buyer who comes into the office twice a month. Some nighttime behavior at conventions can take on the look of a cheap bedroom farce. One friend of mine said, "I go right to my bedroom as soon as I can, lock the door, and pretend I don't hear what I'm hearing out in the hall."

People may act shamelessly or shamefully, depending on how you read it. Besides going to bed with people they wouldn't normally bother with, at conventions people may do it in startling ways. One woman told me that she was about to turn out the light and go to sleep when her roommate for the convention walked in with a man. The roommate was planning on performing coitus in her bed while the roommate was supposed to sleep. On receiving an objection, the roommate remembered what manners she had and took her lover into the bathroom instead.

Another "case" of roomie rudeness occurred when one young male executive asked his gay roommate in the hotel to perform a particular sexual act on him "as a favor." People tend to become rather uncooperative at these conventions, for some reason, and an appeal to their sensibilities doesn't go far. It is best to pretend that all such outrageous activities did not occur, once you have made your own feelings on the matter known.

If you have a large sex drive, you should, if possible, bring along a companion on these trips. That is better than trying to function under one more pressure, or trying to get involved with someone in business that you shouldn't. If sex is available in a discreet situation, then there is no problem. But keeping this particular biological function in check is as important as not getting so drunk you fall down.

BREATHERS

A convention can be a wonderful time, but I once attended one where we were scheduled from 7:30 in the morning right on through till 2:00 A.M. some nights. It was like going to heaven but having to go through hell week first. Some people, using better sense than I, spent an afternoon lolling in the bay and on the beach, sleeping, resting, and getting a nice tan. For myself, a brisk climb up the steep side of a volcano was just the thing to invigorate me after several nights of three-hour naps. I became such a grouchy bear that I actually growled at myself.

If fatigue makes you into a corporate version of the Incredible Hulk, it's much better to take some extra rest time during the trip. It improves business and your disposition overall. You never know whom you will meet, even on these pleasure jaunts, that should be impressed favorably.

FREE FOOD

The food can often be especially good or bad at these functions; the drinks are almost guaranteed to be good; and the hotel may put its best foot forward to encourage a return. I remember one meeting where the hotel kept us supplied with wonderful coffee unavailable in the United States and heaping trays of delicious English tea cakes. It was almost maddening for a sugar and caffeine addict, and the temptation was to eat your way through the whole wonderful weekend, unless, of course, you were taking a break for cocktails.

The temptation is to make a pig of oneself, and to a certain extent there is no reason you should not fully enjoy the abundance of specialties you wouldn't get anywhere else. Remember, however, that uncontrolled appetites are somewhat offensive to people. Don't gorge yourself; or, if you do, be discreet and quiet about it. I watched one man loading his plate, and while he was sitting he called to the waiter, or whoever was near the buffet, to bring him another this or that. We considered chaining him to his pool chair for several hours a day to make sure we would be guaranteed our own meals.

TIME ALONE

When the days and evenings are heavily scheduled, it may become a chore trying to get enough rest. You can resign yourself to a heavy schedule and "relapse," as one woman said, when it's all over. Or you can decline to attend some of the social functions when possible and get away by yourself for a few minutes. This is very important for some people. There is a lot of pressure on most people at these affairs, and by backing off to get your bearings, you may perform more competently during the rest of the proceedings.

DISAPPEARING NAMES

As mentioned earlier, it happens in business that you meet people and in another context either don't remember them at all or forget their names in the pressure of the situation or in the surprise of meeting them. This is one reason that business affairs held away from the office always include name badges to be worn in plain view. They look tacky, but they make it easy to get names right.

Remembering names is a feat that is usually practiced by robust, loud people who have been through some great business-improvement course. Your normal harried exec will probably forget his wife's name at a pressurized office cocktail party.

If you are with someone you must introduce to another and don't remember the name, you can say something like, "Excuse me, you remind me so much of my sister I want to call you her name . . ." and the person will usually save the moment for you by telling you her name.

The best approach is to be very warm and straightforward. Blame your own mind and say, "I've heard so many new names here that I am confused. Please excuse me, but I can't pull your name out of my mind right now." Most people do understand this situation; it is so common that it would be foolish not to take it with good grace.

I always say my name when I meet people I haven't seen in a while, especially at parties. Or, if they start to introduce me hesitantly, I say my name just about the time they would. I find that this helps all the way, since many people on forgetting one person's name also suddenly go blank on the person they are with, and the person will automatically give you his name instead of waiting. It is not rude to preempt an introduction and present yourself.

Name pronunciation is also sometimes a problem even when you have just heard the name spoken. If you have a name that people have trouble with, say it clearly, and if they ask for a repeat, say it more slowly. Don't treat them as children. If there is a common word that sounds like your name, tell them. People I don't know well often think my name is George Bizet, like the composer, and I sometimes use that as a name that rhymes with mine.

It is somewhat more embarrassing to forget that you have ever met a person at all. This can happen if people change their looks, or if you have only seen them in one situation in certain clothes and have come to identify them strictly in one context. I was standing at a bookstore window display once, engrossed in the offerings in the window. I felt someone grasp my arm and say something into my ear. Since it was New York, I turned quickly, sensing immediate danger. I looked into a smiling face, which was obviously not threatening or insane, but in the weirdness of the moment I could not place any familiarity to the features.

The person was waiting for me to say something friendly, and, finally, I had to confess I could not remember who he was. He looked amazed, and immediately I realized that we had worked on a project together only two weeks before that had put us in close proximity for a while. He had left off the glasses and haircut I was used to, and I had only seen him in Levi's and T-shirts up until then. In a suit he looked totally different.

The best thing one can do in these cases is remain polite and state the situation, since it happens so often.

THE QUICK BUSINESS TRIP

Some trips are for business only, involving very short periods of time and no special social events. If you are traveling alone, the only etiquette is to maintain a businesslike approach toward the people you are seeing and spend your evenings exploring the town as you wish. It is always good manners for people in the host town to invite visitors to dinner, if possible, even if there is no more business to be handled that day. After the dinner you can separate, although if you happen to have much in common you may offer to show the person some of the nightlife in your hometown.

It is not required that the visitor accept any invitation for dinner, and he or she may want to explore alone or just get away from the business part of the trip altogether. The same etiquette applies here as anywhere about who pays: the inviting party pays for dinner. It may be that the guest has a large expense account and will insist on taking the check. In this case, it is wrong to refuse. Any time anyone insists on paying a check, it becomes bad manners to argue about it.

It may happen that the traveler is limited in funds but knows you are as well. In this case it is proper to say, "I would like to have dinner with you, but I'm not on an expense account. Would you care to join me anyway?" In such a case it may be necessary for the visitor to take the check stub to verify his expenses, and it is proper for him to do so. If you both need receipts, ask for separate checks or for an additional receipt.

INVITATIONS

It is considered good etiquette to invite an out-of-town co-worker to your home for dinner, or even to stay there instead of at a hotel. This invitation is based on the idea that you have the facilities to make him more comfortable than he would be in a hotel and your food is better than he would get in a restaurant. If you occupy a small apartment, or if you cannot cook well or are not married to a good cook who will want to entertain, then you should make sure he is in the best accommodations possible within the expense account's limitations.

If you live in a town where there are no good restaurants or motels, then you should try to make some comfortable arrangements for the visitor.

The visitor may prefer the time to be alone, no matter what the accommodations, for one reason or another. If so, he should say, thanking the host first, that he would prefer to stay in the hotel, or that he has work to do and would rather do it in the hotel, or say he will be up late and would be more comfortable alone.

If staying at a co-worker's home, you are duty-bound to spend some time after dinner with the host and his or her spouse. If you have work to do or want to sleep early, you may excuse yourself at a certain point and retire. A thank-you note, and even a gift of flowers, is appropriate afterward, or during the stay. It is also appropriate to invite your host and spouse out to dinner one night at least, if there is a good place to dine. If not, a gift is required.

ONE WOMAN, SEVERAL MEN

If after dinner the group wants to go somewhere in the town for some entertainment, it is very bad manners for a group of men to exclude the woman. Remember that it is a business situation, despite the fact that it is nighttime, and all people should be invited to go with the main group. The person may decline, but events that can be handled by both sexes should be considered first, or everyone should go separate ways.

Remember always that on any business trip the business is always the first consideration. You may be itching to see the topless revue, but it is best to set up an evening alone for it when possible, rather than jeopardize your image by insulting someone you work with.

ILLNESS ON THE ROAD

If you become very ill on the road, ask your business associates to recommend a doctor. It is good manners for the hosting associate to keep tabs on the sick visitor and to make sure he or she has anything required in the way of food or medicines. An illness that requires more than one or two days in bed, however, should be handled by a hospital, not in a hotel room. It is an imposition to expect strangers or hotel people to take care of you.

TRAVELING WITH CO-WORKERS

It is not necessary for a man to carry the woman's bags unless it is convenient and he wants to. The woman should have along only as much as she can handle, and so should he.

The person handling expenses pays for everything. In this case etiquette demands that you eat together. You cannot ask for money to eat alone; courtesy turns meals into shared events.

It is important to maintain the same demeanor and manners on the road as you would in the office. Remember that a visitor may feel uncomfortable being alone in the town, and that fact does put you in a position of having to offer to spend some time together. Some people just like to head for their rooms and watch TV and call home before retiring early. Don't turn into someone else in a travel situation. Remain yourself. Be evenly predictable in your behavior and don't suddenly turn into a stranger. It's extremely easy to alienate people in another time zone, and the sour feeling will be difficult to overcome when you get back home.

FINALE

WHY DO WE do it? Why should we expend so much effort just to be nice when so many people make buckets of money not being the least bit nice? The point is not the money; the point is in making everyone's lives—ours included—more worth living. The point of work is survival. The point of work in a civilized society is creative fulfillment, satisfying interaction with our fellow humans, and the creation of communities that are better to live in than, say, battle-fields or jungles.

The easiest social problem to turn around is rudeness. It is as simple as being polite, being considerate, acting as if you care that someone remains in a good mood rather than doing something to put him in a bad humor for the rest of the day.

Of course it's worth it. If it's worth going to work at 8:00 or 9:00 A.M. on a rainy, sleazy day at all, it's worth the extra effort to make it worth spending such a day in the office.

INDEX

Accents, hard to understand, 90–91
Age, discussions of, 44
Aggressiveness, of women, 106
"Air kissing," 88–89
Alcoholism, 96–97
Anger: secretary's, 153–54; when it works, 60–61
Answering services, 199
Arbitration, 58–59
Arriving at a new job, 22–23
Authority, women at work and, 105
Avoidance (phone call) game, 200–201

Back stabbers, 57
Bad seeds, 86–87
Beard growing, 76
Birthday wishes, 93
Body odor, 73
Borrowers and "bummers," 64
Boss, 167–87; apology from, 181–82; compliments, 173; criticism, 184; criticizing friends, 177–78; emotional outbursts, 174–75; employee's personal problems and, 179–80; entertaining at home, 224–25; family members of, 185–86, 186–87; fear of firing, 169–70; flattery and, 173–74; hiring friends,

177–78; importance of objectivity, 176; inability to communicate, 180–81; ingratiating people and, 178–79; leading by example, 172–73; and province of managers, 184–85; rudeness, 183–84; secretary's covering for, 54, 154, 155, 160–161, 196–97; secretary's phoning for, 195; self-critique, 170–72; sexual advances by, 131–33; shopping for, 146; talking back to, 182–83; unreasonable, 169; use of firing as a weapon, 168–69
Business calling card, 93–94
Business lunch, 208–24; alcohol, 221; avoiding, 219–20; at the bar, 211; boorish guest behavior, 218; cancelling, 210; check, 211–12; and close restaurant tables, 222–23; coatroom, 217; emergencies, 221; and expense account cut, 214–15; extravagance, 214; going dutch, 213–14; invitation, 209; lateness, 210; nondrinkers, 219; personal needs, 216; poachers, 223–24; procedure, 215–16; at the restaurant, 210–11; separating after the meal,

251

217–18; small talk, 220; tip and bill arrangements beforehand, 212–13; tipping, 216–17

Chair pullers, 110–12
Christmas decorations, 42
Cigarette bummers, 64
Cigarette lighting, 110
Clothes: dress codes, 68–70; free lancing and, 234; inappropriateness of dress, 74–75, 75–76; job interview, 19–20; overdressing for the occasion, 76; repairs, 78; sexy, 77–78
Cocaine and marijuana, 97–99
Coffee making, secretary and, 146
Colognes or perfumes, 73–74
Compliments, 79, 173; to a woman's work, 109
Condolences, 93
Contagious disease, 95–96
Covering: for the boss, 54, 154, 155, 160–61; for a co-worker, 53–54
Criticism, 184

Decor, 42
Dirty jokes, 82–83
Dress. See Clothes
Drugs, 97–99

Elevators, 112–14
Entertaining at home, 224–32; boss and, 224–25; butlers and bartenders, 227–28; cooking, 226–27; embarrassing situations, 231; and pets, 231–32; setting limits, 230–31; spouse and, 228–29; what to hide from guests, 230; whom to invite, 229
Ethnic jokes, 83–84

Familiarity, between boss and secretary, 147–48

Femininity and business success, 102
Firing: fear of, 169–70; as a weapon, 168–69
First names, 159
Fist fights, 57–58
Flattery, boss and, 173–74
Forbes, Malcolm S., 183–84
Foreign accents, 90–91
Four-letter words, 82
Freebies and discounts, 61–62
Free-lancers, 233–37; attitudes of, 234–35; clothing for, 234; deadlines and payment, 233–34; expenses, 235–40; "fast" requests, 237; guarantees, 236; scouting for new contacts, 236–37

Gay people, 139–40
Getting along. See Office interaction
Gifts, to secretaries, 155–57
Goof-offs, 53
Gossip, 45–46; about romantic affairs, 143
Grapevines, 45–46
Guests, escorting, 48
Guilt without sex, 138
Gum chewing, 67–68

Handicaps, working with, 89–90
Handshakes, 87–88
Hanukkah decorations, 42
Harassment, sexual, 133–34
Hatred, 36–37
Housecleaning the staff, 31

Illness: contagious, 95–96; and termination of employment, 94
Income: keeping quiet about, 23–24; promised raises, 25; and worth, 24–25
Inherited staff, 23

Inner transfer, 28–29
Interruptions, telephone, 202–4
Interviews, 17–19, 21–22
Introductions, 108
Invitations: business lunch, 209; travel, 245–46

Jokes, 82–84

Kissing, 88, 123–26

Language and diction, 81–82
Lateness: business lunch, 210; at work, 52–53
Lawsuits, 32
Leaving the company, 29–30
Letting go, 29
Loans, 63, 64
Love. *See* Romantic possibilities and love affairs
Lover, promotion of, 142
Lying, on the telephone, 196–97

Makeup, 67
Male bonding, 106
Marijuana, 97–99
Married couples: both working within the company, 141–42
Married person, sexual overture by, 122–23
Meddlers, 46–47
Message machines, 199
Messages, telephone, 198–99
Money matters, questions not to ask, 43–44
Moodiness, 59–60
Moving on, 30

Nail clippers, 67
Names: importance of, 85–86; using secretary's, 158–59
Nosiness, 42–44
Notes: birthday wishes, 93; business calling cards, 93–94; condolences, 93; of congratulations, 92–93; thank-you, 91–92

Office interaction, 33–64; age and weight discussions, 44; anger and when it works, 60–61; arbitration, 58–59; back stabbers, 57; being offered boss's job, 54–55; borrowers and "bummers," 64; children and pets, 49–50; chronic goof-offs, 53; covering up, 53–54; dealing with strangers, 47–49; decor, 42; fist fights and arguments, 57–58; freebies and discounts, 61–62; gossip, 45–46; hatred, 36–37; lateness or early departures, 52–53; loans and getting money back, 63–64; meddlers, 46–47; moodiness, 59–60; nosiness and questions not to ask, 42–44; petty-cash disbursements, 63; radio playing, 37–38; scapegoats, 55–56; schmoozers, singers, and kibitzers, 51; smokers and non-smokers, 38–41; spaces, 34–35; unannounced visitors, 50–51; unwanted talkers, 51–52
Office roommates, 35–36
One-night stands, 126–27; 135–36

Passes: from the boss's wife (or family), 140; handling, 134–35
Paternalism, toward women, 103–5
Personal calls, 204
Personal image, 65–99; alcoholism, 96–97; baggy trousers, 74–75; body odor, 73; "brownnosing," 79–80; compliments, 79; dress codes, 68–70; 75–76; drugs, 97–99; foreign accents, 90–91; four-letter words, 82; handshake, 87–88; hello/goodbye, 78;

illness, 95–96; inappropriateness of dress, 75–76; jokes, 82–84; kisses, 88–89; language and diction, 81–82; names and pronunciation, 85–86; notes and calling cards, 91–94; people with whom you can't get along, 86–87; piggish behavior, 66–68; put-downs, 84–85; repairs to torn clothing, 78; scents and fragrances, 73–74; sexy clothing, 77–78; smiles, 80–81; taboos, 70–72; working with handicaps, 89–90

Personal problems (in a secretary/boss relationship), 157–58

Pests (job applicants), 20–21

Petty-cash disbursements, 63

Piggish behavior, 66–68

Predators, sexual, 121–22

Private telephone lines, 199–200

Profanities, 106–7

Promotion, versus hiring from the outside, 27–28

Puppy love, 143

Put-downs, 84–85

Quitting, 31

Radio playing, 37–38

Reception areas, 41

Receptionists, 162–66; greeting area, 162–64; qualifications, 164–65

Resentment, secretary's, 153–54

Résumé, 15–17

Returning telephone calls, 194–95

Revolving doors, 112–14

Romantic possibilities and love affairs, 116–43; boss's wife and kids, 140; gay people, 139–40; gossip, 143; guilt without sex, 138; handling passes, 134–35; harassment, 133–34; how to avoid a kiss, 125–26; how to handle the lovers, 118–20; inappropriate demonstrations of affection, 125; kissing, 123–25; love affairs, 127–30; married couples (working in the company), 141–42; married persons and sexual overtures, 122–23; one-night stands, 126–27, 135–36; pattern of, 129–30; predators, 121–22; promoting the lover, 142; puppy love, 143; secretary covering for boss's sexual affairs, 154, 155; sex in the office, 136–38; sexual advances by the boss, 131–33; sexual conquistadors, 130–31; unmarried couples, 140

Roommates (office), 35–36

Rudeness: boss's, 183–84; on the telephone, 201–2

Salary levels, 24–25

Salary raise: asking for, 25–27; promised but not materialized, 25

Scapegoats, 55–56; bowing out gracefully, 56

Scents and fragrances, 73–74

Schmoozers, singers, and kibitzers, 51

Secretaries, 144–66; amenities expected by, 149–50; anger and resentment of, 153–54; complaints from, 148–49; covering for the boss, 154, 155, 160–61, 196–97; executive's personal social setup and, 151–52; expectations, 145–47; familiarity between bosses and, 147–48; gifts to, 155–57; image and self-image, 161–62; kinds of, 148; personal problems, 157–58;

phoning for the boss, 195; politeness to co-workers, 159–60; receptionist, 162–66; social relationship with the boss, 151–53; using the names of, 158–59

Sex: at a convention, 241–42; in the office, 136–38

Sexual harassment, 133–34

Sexy clothing, 77–78

Smiles, 80–81

Smokers and nonsmokers, 38–41

Space, sharing with others, 34–35

Staff, revaluating, 31

Taboos, personal image, 70–72

Tardiness, 52–53

Telephone etiquette, 188–207; advance preparation, 205; answering services, 199; avoidance game, 200–201; avoiding home calls, 206–7; covering the line, 192; food or drink when talking, 204–5; getting through, 193–94; on hold and forgotten, 191; how to answer, 191; interruptions, 202–4; leaving messages, 198–99; lying, 196–97; message machines, 199; music on the hold line, 190–91; personal calls, 204; personal references and, 193; person's time and, 205–6; placing call for first time, 192–93; private lines, 199–200; returning calls, 194–95; ringing more than three times, 189–90; secretary-for-boss calls, 195; "thank you," 197; unknown callers, 196; voice mannerisms, 197–98; when to be rude, 201–2; when to help, 202

Temps, politeness to, 47

Thank-you notes, 91–92

Tipping, lunch etiquette, 216–17

Touching, 87–88

Travel, 238–47; congeniality, 240; with co-workers, 247; free food and, 242–43; getting there, 239; illness on the road, 247; invitations, 245–46; one woman, several men, 246; quick business trip, 245; remembering names and people, 243–45; sex and, 241–42; strangeness, 240; time alone, 243

Two weeks' notice, 31–32

Unmarried couples, 140, 141

Unwanted talkers, 51–52

Visitors: in the boss's office, 49; children and pets, 49–50; guests, 48; schmoozers, singers, and kibitzers, 51; stranger in middle of the office, 48; temps, 47; unexpected, 50–51

Voice mannerisms, 197–98

Weight, discussions of, 44

Women at work, 100–15; aggressiveness, 106; approaches men take, 101; authority, 105; chair pullers, 110–12; cigarette lighting, 110; compliments, 109; exclusion of from a discussion, 106, 108; femininity, 102; good manners versus condescension, 109–10; introductions, 108; paternalism, 103–5; social functions and conventions, 107–8; vulgar language, 106–7

Yelling arguments, 58

Yentas, 46–47

ABOUT THE AUTHOR

George Mazzei worked in the corporate world for some fifteen years as an editor and writer and served as Managing Editor of *Gentleman's Quarterly Magazine* for eight years. He is also the author of *Shaping Up*, a book on putting together your own gym program. Currently he is a free-lance writer, living in New York City.